# THE HOLY SPIRIT AND SUPERNATURAL POWER

Michael Nwaduba

Grosvenor House
Publishing Limited

All rights reserved
Copyright © Michael Nwaduba, 2023

The right of Michael Nwaduba to be identified as the author of this work has been asserted in accordance with Section 78 of the Copyright, Designs and Patents Act 1988

The book cover is copyright to Michael Nwaduba

This book is published by
Grosvenor House Publishing Ltd
Link House
140 The Broadway, Tolworth, Surrey, KT6 7HT.
www.grosvenorhousepublishing.co.uk

This book is sold subject to the conditions that it shall not, by way of trade or otherwise, be lent, resold, hired out or otherwise circulated without the author's or publisher's prior consent in any form of binding or cover other than that in which it is published and without a similar condition including this condition being imposed on the subsequent purchaser.

NOTE:
The information and views expressed in this book by the author should not be used as a substitute for professional medical advice or treatment, always consult your doctor. Any use of the information in this book is entirely at the reader's discretion and risk. The author or publisher cannot be held liable for any loss, claim, or damages arising out of the use or misuse of the suggestions made in this book.

A CIP record for this book
is available from the British Library

Paperback ISBN 978-1-80381-647-0
Hardback ISBN 978-1-80381-648-7
eBook ISBN 978-1-80381-649-4

# Contents

| | | |
|---|---|---|
| Preface | | v |
| 1 | The Holy Spirit is a Person | 1 |
| 2 | The Holy Spirit is God | 28 |
| 3 | The Names and Works of the Holy Spirit | 35 |
| 4 | The Human Spirit, Soul, and Body | 58 |
| 5 | The Supernatural Realm | 87 |
| 6 | The Symbols of the Holy Spirit | 108 |
| 7 | Salvation and Indwelling of the Holy Spirit | 116 |
| 8 | Infilling of the Holy Spirit | 134 |
| 9 | The Holy Spirit Empowerment | 142 |
| 10 | The Nine Gifts of the Holy Spirit | 177 |
| 11 | The Nine Fruit of the Holy Spirit | 204 |
| 12 | Intimacy with the Holy Spirit | 217 |
| Spread the Good News | | 227 |
| Bibliography | | 228 |

# Preface

Your time has indeed come to be filled with the Holy Spirit and to start manifesting the power and the glory of God. The fact that you made the decision to read this book is a clear evidence that you desire a relationship to know the Holy Spirit more intimately, connect to His supernatural power, and then start manifesting the power with ease.

The good news I have for you is that you have made the right decision to read this book. The Holy Spirit Himself is our great teacher, and He inspired me to write this book which carries the anointing of the Holy Spirit to permeate your spirit, soul, and body, and fill you with power, love, peace, and joy as you read. Therefore, open your heart to receive the Word of God, wrapped with wisdom to transform and promote you to a glorious transcendent realm.

Get ready for miracles that will begin to happen to you as you intentionally, and deliberately commence endless fellowship with this lovely, gentle Holy Spirit. You will live to appreciate Him more and more, and also testify of His goodness and mercy.

When you start walking closely with the Holy Spirit in a more intimate relationship, you will discover that you will begin to pay attention to details, involving Him in your affairs, and decisions. He is our Helper, Comforter, Advocate, Counsellor, Standby, Strengthener, Intercessor, plus much more. The Holy Spirit, or Holy Ghost our Helper is called *Parakletos* in Greek.

As powerful, lovely, and gentle as the Holy Spirit is, He seems to be the least known, and acknowledged in the church, and body of Christ among the Trinity or Godhead, made up of the Father God,

Son Jesus Christ, and the Holy Spirit. The purpose of this book is to:

- Bring Him to your awareness and consciousness
- Get you to be filled with the Holy Spirit
- Encourage you to have a regular well intentioned relationship with Him
- Get you to acknowledge Him at all times and stop ignoring Him
- Encourage you to deliberately create the right atmosphere to be with Him
- Isolate yourself regularly to have fellowship, and intimacy with Him
- Get you to know the secrets to enable you align yourself with Him
- Get you to hunger and thirst for His presence more and more
- Encourage you to have self-discipline not to grieve Him
- Start manifesting the power and glory of God with ease and regularly

Right from Genesis, the Holy Spirit was there in creation to display His awesome power that He is known for. The Bible says in:

*Genesis 1:1-2*

¹ *In the beginning God created the heaven and the earth.*

² *And the earth was without form, and void; and darkness was upon the face of the deep. And the Spirit of God moved upon the face of the waters.*

Verse 2 above confirms that the Spirit of God was present right from the beginning to help during creation. This shows that the Holy Spirit is so powerful and important.

*Genesis 1:26*

*And God said, Let us make man in our image, after our likeness: and let them have dominion over the fish of the sea, and over the fowl of the air, and over the cattle, and over all the earth, and over every creeping thing that creepeth upon the earth.*

The above scripture further confirms that the Holy Spirit was also present during the creation of man. This statement by God, "*Let us ...,*" is an indication of the Trinity or Godhead coming together and the Holy Spirit is part of them. *Job 33:4* also says the Holy Spirit made us stating, "*The Spirit of God hath made me, and the breath of the Almighty hath given me life.*"

Apart from the wonderful acts of creation we have seen above performed by the Holy Spirit, we also have records in the Old Testament to prove that the Holy Spirit empowered men whenever they had special assignments to perform, or when they held certain office like king, prophet, judge, or priest. Usually, the Holy Spirit came *upon* these men in the **Old Testament**. Examples include:

## BEZALEEL

*Exodus 31:1-3*

[1] *And the LORD spake unto Moses, saying.*

[2] *See, I have called by name Bezaleel the son of Uri, the son of Hur, of the tribe of Judah.*

[3] *And I have filled him with the spirit of God, in wisdom, and in understanding, and in knowledge, and in all manner of workmanship.*

Verse 3 above clearly tells us that Bezaleel was filled with the Spirit of God. This is Holy Spirit empowerment to function excellently in all manner of workmanship.

## GIDEON

*Judges 6:34*

*But the Spirit of the LORD came upon Gideon, and he blew a trumpet; and Abiezer was gathered after him.*

The Spirit of the Lord came upon Gideon to empower him to lead the Israelites against the Midianites. He accomplished this task with just 300 men.

## SAMSON

*Judges 14:6*

*And the Spirit of the LORD came mightily upon him, and he rent him as he would have rent a kid, and he had nothing in his hand: but he told not his father or his mother what he had done.*

The Spirit of the LORD came mightily upon Samson and he killed a lion.

## DAVID

*Psalms 51:11*

*Cast me not away from thy presence; and take not thy holy spirit from me.*

David valued the Holy Spirit so much that he had to pray to God not to take Him away from him when he committed adultery with Bathsheba.

In the Old Testament, the Holy Spirit usually came *upon* people. This means that the Holy Spirit can come and go. He did not abide in them permanently. No wonder King David prayed to God in *Psalms 51:11*, "*Cast me not away from thy presence; and take not thy holy spirit from me.*" To buttress this point, read what the Bible says about King Saul and the Holy Spirit in:

## 1 Samuel 16:14

*But the Spirit of the LORD departed from Saul, and an evil spirit from the LORD troubled him.*

Moving on to the **New Testament,** we see more displays of the awesome power of the Holy Spirit in action. Jesus promised that after His death, resurrection, and ascension, the Holy Spirit, another Comforter of His kind (*Allos Parakletos*), will be sent to abide with us forever. Hallelujah! He said He will not leave us as orphans. Therefore, it is expedient that He goes to be seated at the right hand of the Father in Heaven.

## John 14:16-18

*[16] And I will pray the Father, and he shall give you another Comforter, that he may abide with you for ever;*

*[17] Even the Spirit of truth; whom the world cannot receive, because it seeth him not, neither knoweth him: but ye know him; for he dwelleth with you, and shall be in you.*

*[18] I will not leave you comfortless: I will come to you.*

## John 14:26

*But the Comforter, which is the Holy Ghost, whom the Father will send in my name, he shall teach you all things, and bring all things to your remembrance, whatsoever I have said unto you.*

## John 16:13

*Howbeit when he, the Spirit of truth, is come, he will guide you into all truth: for he shall not speak of himself; but whatsoever he shall hear, that shall he speak: and he will shew you things to come.*

On the day of Pentecost, the Holy Spirit manifested in great measure and filled the disciples and they all spoke with other tongues. Praise God!

*Acts 2:1-4*

¹ *And when the day of Pentecost was fully come, they were all with one accord in one place.*

² *And suddenly there came a sound from heaven as of a rushing mighty wind, and it filled all the house where they were sitting.*

³ *And there appeared unto them cloven tongues like as of fire, and it sat upon each of them.*

⁴ *And they were all filled with the Holy Ghost, and began to speak with other tongues, as the Spirit gave them utterance.*

In the *New Testament*, all born again believers have the Holy Spirit *indwelling* in them forever. The Holy Spirit is irrevocable, but He can be grieved, ignored, or made dormant by a believer. Therefore, the saints of God must ensure they are filled with the Holy Spirit just like:

## PETER

*Acts 4:8*

*Then Peter, filled with the Holy Ghost, said unto them, Ye rulers of the people, and elders of Israel.*

Peter was filled with the Holy Spirit and declared the Word of God with all boldness in the Sanhedrin.

## PAUL

*Acts 9:17*

*And Ananias went his way, and entered into the house; and putting his hands on him said, Brother Saul, the Lord, even Jesus, that appeared unto thee in the way as thou camest, hath sent me, that thou mightest receive thy sight, and be filled with the Holy Ghost.*

Apostle Paul was filled with the Holy Spirit before he started preaching the gospel.

## JESUS

*John 3:34*

*For he whom God hath sent speaketh the words of God: for God giveth not the Spirit by measure unto him.*

God gave Jesus the Holy Spirit without measure. Unlimited!

Today, born again Christians have a regenerated spirit, and the Holy Spirit dwells within them. Our body is the temple of the Holy Spirit – 1 Corinthians 6:19.

Before marriage, a prospective couple begins dating. After a satisfactory period of courtship, they proceed further and deeper with their relationship as the bridegroom pays the dowry, and a wedding is conducted which will go even deeper with intercourse and consummation. You obviously engage in intercourse with your spouse in a secret place, conducive atmosphere, and not in a hurry or openly. We are to do the same thing with the Holy Spirit, by having fellowship and communion with Him. This is called *Koinonia* in Greek. Jesus Christ is our bridegroom, and we are His bride, as born again Christians, and the Holy Spirit is our administrator.

I would like to emphasize in this preface section of this book a very important non-negotiable secret you need to know about the Holy Ghost power. It is the fact that you must be prepared to isolate yourself, pay the price, through self-discipline, and dwell in the secret place often carrying out spiritual exercises such as Bible study, meditation, fasting, prayers, praise, worship, reading Christian books etc in order to hear Him, know Him, and be infused with His supernatural power. This power takes a long time to attain. It's not automatic, neither is it by luck, nor by abracadabra. If you are too busy not to spend your quality time with the Holy Spirit, then forget about supernatural power. You must also be prepared to be *obedient* to the Word of God, and enthrone, honour, and revere Him above all things in your life. Now that you know these things, happy are ye if you do them – John 13:17.

Before our Lord Jesus Christ, our Christian model was anointed with Holy Ghost power, He had to pay the price, and went through the process as follows: He was conceived by the power of the Holy Spirit – Luke 1:35; He was filled with the Holy Spirit immediately after water baptism – Matthew 3:16-17, Luke 3:21-22; led by the Holy Spirit into the wilderness in isolation to be tempted for 40 days while He fasted – Luke 4:1-2. Afterwards, the Bible says in:

## Luke 4:14

*And Jesus returned in the power of the Spirit into Galilee: and there went out a fame of him through all the region round about.*

This is the biblical pattern for acquiring supernatural Holy Ghost power. Therefore, if you desire this power, pay the price, go through the process, and you will be endued with power.

By the time you finish reading this book and also commence a serious relationship with the Holy Spirit, you will get to realize that the Holy Spirit is more real than people around you even though He is invisible, and intangible because you will begin to communicate with Him more frequently, and intimately. You will walk with Him, feel Him, and laugh with Him. You will become very conscious of Him. The Holy Spirit is real. He is your best Friend!

I confidently guarantee you one thing. When you sincerely and wholeheartedly partner with the Holy Spirit in any and everything you do in life, consider it excellent and a huge success. Partner with Him! You will always be a winner, overcomer, and more than a conqueror when you do.

My prayer for you as you read this book is *1 Thessalonians 5:23*:

> *"And the very God of peace sanctify you wholly; and I pray God your whole spirit and soul and body be preserved blameless unto the coming of our Lord Jesus Christ."* God bless you abundantly in Jesus' name. Amen!

MICHAEL NWADUBA

# CHAPTER ONE

# THE HOLY SPIRIT IS A PERSON

## Brief background information about the Holy Spirit

The Holy Spirit is a person. He has a mind, emotions, and will (MEW). We will look at these characteristics in line with the scriptures.

The Holy Spirit, also known as the "Holy Ghost" or simply "Spirit" is indeed holy and should be treated with holiness and reverence. The Hebrew word for "Holy" is *Qados*[1] which simply means to set apart for a specific purpose. The Greek word for "Holy" is *Hagiasmos*[2] as a noun, and *Hagiazo*[3] as a verb.

The Hebrew word for "Spirit" is *Ruah*[4], and this also means "breath", "wind" or "mind". The Greek word for "Spirit" is *Pneuma*[5], and this also means "breath" or "wind". These are expressed in John 4:24, Genesis 2:7, Job 33:4, and John 3:8.

The Holy Spirit is part of the Trinity or Godhead. This refers to three persons in one. That is, God the Father, Jesus Christ the Son, and the Holy Spirit. They are each God on their own, capable of individual existence, as well as mutual co-existence.

Note that the Holy Spirit is invisible, intangible, and eternal or everlasting in nature. Is it therefore not a mystery that the Holy Spirit appears to be real, so much that one can have an intimate relationship with Him? Well, the Holy Spirit is not a mystery to Spirit filled believers, who walk by faith and not by sight, and that's why they can truly have a relationship with Him.

The Holy Spirit is associated with different symbols and metaphors such as water, fire, oil, wind, wine, dove, cloud, aprons, handkerchiefs, communion, and born again Christians. We will discuss this further in chapter six.

The Bible was written by men inspired by the Holy Spirit. Therefore, in order to deliver a true and concrete account of this subject, I will be supporting this write up with biblical references. *King James Version (KJV)* appears to be the most popular and widely used version. Therefore, that will be my main version, and I will indicate whenever I use other translations. See 2 Timothy 3:16 and 2 Peter 1:21.

The Holy Spirit is a person, and therefore, should always be referred to with the pronoun 'He' or 'Him'. The Holy Spirit is not 'It', and should never be referred to as such. Jesus Himself referred to the Holy Spirit as 'He' or 'Him'. This is what Jesus said about the Holy Spirit in:

## John 14:16-17

[16] *And I will pray the Father, and he shall give you another Comforter, that he may abide with you for ever;*

[17] *Even the Spirit of truth; whom the world cannot receive, because it seeth him not, neither knoweth him: but ye know him; for he dwelleth with you, and shall be in you.* (Underline mine)

The King James Version (KJV) referred to the Holy Spirit as 'he' and 'him' instead of 'He' and 'Him' in the above verse. This does not appear to be right because the Holy Spirit is God and therefore should be written with capital letters 'He' and 'Him'. See the New King James Version (NKJV) for the correct rendition.

The "Holy Spirit" or "Holy Ghost" or "Spirit", must always be written with capital "H and S", "H and G" or 'S'. On the other hand, the human spirit should always be written with a small letter 's.' Evil spirits should also be written with small letter 's' in the Bible. For illustration purpose, let's consider the following scriptures again:

## Psalms 51:11

*Cast me not away from thy presence; and take not thy <u>holy spirit</u> from me.* (Underline mine)

The King James Version (KJV) referred to the Holy Spirit as "holy spirit" in the above scripture instead of "Holy Spirit" and it ought not to be so because the Holy Spirit is a person, and also God. The "H and S" should have been in capital letters.

Can you imagine the name of a person called "Howard Smith" being written as "howard smith," or the name of "Jesus Christ" written as "jesus christ"? Is this right? No! This is how the New International Version (NIV) stated it in:

## Psalms 51:11

*Do not cast me from your presence or take your <u>Holy Spirit</u> from me. (NIV)* (Underline mine)

Other translations – AMPC, NKJV, NLT, NAS etc also put down Psalm 51:11 as "Holy Spirit."

Let's look at another scripture:

## Exodus 31:1-3

*[1] And the LORD spake unto Moses, saying,*

*[2] See, I have called by name Bezaleel the son of Uri, the son of Hur, of the tribe of Judah:*

*[3] And I have <u>filled</u> him with the <u>spirit of God</u>, in wisdom, and in understanding, and in knowledge, and in all manner of workmanship,* (Underline mine)

Note that in the Old Testament, the pattern is that the Holy Spirit usually came *upon* people, but verse 3 above of the (KJV) tells us that Bezaleel was *filled* with the Holy Spirit. The underlined "spirit of God" in the same verse 3 above does not appear to be right. It should have been written with capital letter 'S' like this, "Spirit of God" because the Spirit is of God. This is how the New International Version (NIV) put it:

*Exodus 31:3*

*and I have filled him with the <u>Spirit of God</u>, with wisdom, with understanding, with knowledge and with all kinds of skills— (NIV)* (Underline mine)

Other translations - AMPC, NKJV, NLT, NAS etc also put down Exodus 31:3 as "Spirit of God."

Let's look at another scripture:

*1 Samuel 16:14*

*But the <u>Spirit of the LORD</u> departed from Saul, and an <u>evil spirit from the LORD</u> troubled him.* (Underline mine)

The underlined "*Spirit of the LORD*" in the above scripture of 1 Samuel 16:14 (KJV) is correct with capital letter 'S' because the Spirit is of the LORD. The "*evil spirit from the LORD*" underlined above is also correct with small letter 's' because the spirit is *negative* or evil even though it is also from the LORD. *Please note this important point because it's going to come up again and again in this book.* AMPC, NKJV, NLT, NAS, NIV etc also put down the "Spirit of the LORD" and "evil spirit" in the same way as (KJV) and this shows it is correct. The reason why I brought it up is because I want you to be aware and note the "Spirit" and "spirit" and how they were used in the verse.

Henceforth, it is important to always pay attention to whether your Bible used "Spirit" or "spirit" in a verse, or passage in order to be sure of the kind of spirit that is being referred to. I have observed that sometimes different translations use them *interchangeably*, and it ought not to be so especially when you really need to be sure of the kind of spirit the Bible is referring to. You should be able to know straightaway if your Bible is talking about *Holy Spirit, human spirit, or evil spirit.* Note that the Holy Spirit is superior to every other spirit. That is why the "Spirit" comes with a capital letter 'S', and other spirits with small letter 's'.

What's the *solution* to deal with this sort of situation if it arises or you are not sure? *First*, read the pre and post text around the scripture in context. This will enable you to comprehend more. *Second*, compare the verse or verses in context with other translations of the Bible as we just did above to see how it was used. *Third*, check out your Hebrew and Greek dictionary to see how it was used originally. *Fourth*, you can even check things out on the internet with your mobile. Handy! *Fifth*, meditate on the scripture and ask the Holy Spirit to clarify to you the correct usage because the Holy Spirit inspired men to write the Bible. He is our great teacher, and He knows the answer.

## THE HOLY SPIRIT IS A PERSON

CHARACTERISTICS – The Holy Spirit has a mind, emotions, and will (MEW). Let's discuss these features, plus much more.

MIND – The Holy Spirit has a mind, and therefore able to know things, and make decisions, because He is intelligent.

## 1. The Holy Spirit has a mind

*Romans 8:26-27*

[26] *Likewise the Spirit also helpeth our infirmities: for we know not what we should pray for as we ought: but the Spirit itself maketh intercession for us with groanings which cannot be uttered.*

*²⁷ And he that searcheth the hearts knoweth what is the <u>mind of the Spirit</u>, because he maketh intercession for the saints according to the will of God.* (Underline mine)

As I pointed out before, the Holy Spirit should not be addressed with the pronoun 'It' but, 'He' or 'Him'. Therefore, the underlined "itself" in verse 26 *above* should have been "Himself". See how the New King James Version (NKJV) puts it below.

*Romans 8:26 (NKJV)*

*Likewise the Spirit also helps in our weaknesses. For we do not know what we should pray for as we ought, but the Spirit <u>Himself</u> makes intercession* [a]*for us with groanings which cannot be uttered.* (Underline mine)

Verse 27 above tells us about the mind of the Spirit. Only a person has the capacity to think, know things, and make decisions which the Holy Spirit does. This quality puts the Holy Spirit in the same position as a person.

## 2. The Holy Spirit makes intercession for us

Romans 8:26 above tells us that the Holy Spirit makes intercession for us with groaning, and this is the character of a person. To groan for us during intercession is a deep expression of how much the Holy Spirit cares. The Holy Spirit helps our infirmities. Verse 27 also clearly tells us that He makes intercession for us according to the will of God. To make intercession according to the will of God is talking about interceding in line with the scriptures, our assignment, and to bring us in alignment with God. When the Holy Spirit intercedes for you, He does it with precision to ensure that He hits the target. He does not pray amiss. You should be encouraged and excited to know that you have a trusted partner interceding for you, and helping your infirmities. Heavenly Father, I thank you because the Holy Spirit is ever interceding for us. We receive positive answers to all our prayer requests, and to also give testimonies in Jesus' name. Amen!

Is the assurance that the Holy Spirit is interceding for us a license to sit back and start lazing about and stop praying? No! We must not abuse this privilege and favor and stop praying. As a matter of fact, as we also pray for ourselves, the Holy Spirit prays in us and through us. Therefore, it can also be a partnership intercession whereby the *Holy Spirit interacts* with our *human spirit* during intercession. This is why I will encourage believers to pray in tongues, which is also known as praying in the unknown language, or in the Spirit. This exercise will edify you. Praise God! *Jude 1:20* says, *"But ye, beloved, building up yourselves on your most holy faith, praying in the Holy Ghost."* Pray in the Holy Ghost and start seeing signs, wonders, and miracles happen in your life in Jesus' name. Amen! Remember to always feed yourself with the Word of God because a combination of the sword of the Spirit and the Holy Spirit in prayers does produce great results.

## 3. The Holy Spirit searches and knows the deep things of God

The Bible says in *1 Corinthians 2:9-11:*

⁹ *But as it is written, Eye hath not seen, nor ear heard, neither have entered into the heart of man, the things which God hath prepared for them that love him.*

¹⁰ *But God hath <u>revealed</u> them unto us by his <u>Spirit</u>: for the <u>Spirit</u> searcheth all things, yea, the deep things of God.*

¹¹ *For what man <u>knoweth</u> the things of a man, save the <u>spirit of man</u> which is in him? even so the things of God <u>knoweth</u> no man, but the <u>Spirit of God</u>.* (Underline mine)

The Word of God says in verse 10 above that the Holy Spirit searcheth all things including the deep things of God. He also reveals things. Verse 11 says that He knows the things of God which no man knows. This shows the Holy Spirit is intelligent, and this is a demonstration of the character of a person. You need to be a person to be able to know the things of God. Therefore, the Holy Spirit is a person.

In verse 10 above, I underlined two "Spirit" to let you know that these two with capital letters 'S' are talking about the Holy Spirit. I also underlined "spirit of man" in verse 11 with small letter 's' for "spirit." The reason why I did this is to draw your attention to the fact that they are not the same. The first one is the Holy Spirit, and the second one is the human spirit. They are different. How does God reveal things to us? One sure way He does it is through interaction between the Holy Spirit and the human spirit. The Bible says in:

## Romans 8:16

*The <u>Spirit itself</u> beareth witness with our <u>spirit</u>, that we are the children of God:* (Underline mine). This scripture makes it clear that the Holy Spirit Himself interacts with our human spirit. He bears witness with our spirit that we are born again children of God to be favored and blessed.

He does a similar thing to speak to us. God rarely speaks audibly. Instead, the Holy Spirit will interact or speak to our human spirit and we will discern His thoughts through our mind. Sharpen your human spirit. How? Do more Bible study, meditation, prayers, fasting, praise, and worship.

What is hidden, unknown, or lost that you are searching for? Are they simple or deep things? Ask the Holy Spirit to reveal to you those things, and trust and depend on Him to let you know the answers. He knows even the deep things of God. I have been in situations where I am looking for something like my house keys, a document, money, or how to tackle a problem. I simply ask the Holy Spirit and He will reveal the answer to me sometimes speedily. Amazing! Try doing the same thing even in small things and you will see the Holy Spirit in action. The Holy Spirit is a person. Be conscious of His presence. Always create the right conducive *atmosphere* to welcome, and acknowledge Him at all times in your affairs. Surrender everything to Him, kill your pride, and enthrone Him to first place in all you do.

**EMOTIONS** – The Holy Spirit expresses emotions. For example, the Holy Spirit can be grieved, and vexed. And if He can be made angry and sorrowful, then He can also be made happy, joyful, and loving. This is also another character of the Holy Spirit which goes to prove that He is indeed a person.

## 4. The Holy Spirit can be grieved

*Ephesians 4:30*

*And grieve not the holy Spirit of God, whereby ye are sealed unto the day of redemption.*

The above scripture clearly urges believers not to grieve the Holy Spirit. To grieve is to be in pain, unhappy, and sorrowful. How can a believer grieve the Holy Spirit? Some of the ways are: *First*, by ignoring Him. *Second*, by being blasphemous. *Third*, by adopting a lifestyle of sin engaging in lying, debauchery, covetousness, wickedness etc. *Fourth*, engaging in pride and idolatry.

## 5. There can be a rebellion and vexation of the Holy Spirit

The Bible says in:

*Isaiah 63:10*

*But they rebelled, and vexed his holy Spirit: therefore he was turned to be their enemy, and he fought against them.*

There can be a rebellion against the Holy Spirit. He can also be vexed as we see in the above scripture. To do this will make Him angry, and the above scripture says those who do so will be fought. Who can fight God and win? Nobody! Therefore, it is better to submit yourself to the Holy Spirit, be humble, and cooperate with Him in all things. Accept the Holy Spirit and embrace Him wholeheartedly as your best Friend.

## 6. The Holy Spirit loves and He is joyful

In this section, we will see that the Holy Spirit also expresses positive emotions like love, peace, and joy. This shows He is a person.

*Romans 5:5*

*And hope maketh not ashamed; because the love of God is shed abroad in our hearts by the Holy Ghost which is given unto us.*

The above scripture clearly tells us that the love of God is shed abroad in our hearts by the Holy Ghost. This shows the Holy Spirit is indeed love because for Him to shed love in our heart, He must have love. You can't give what you don't have.

*Romans 14:17*

*For the kingdom of God is not meat and drink; but righteousness, and <u>peace, and joy in the Holy Ghost</u>.* (Underline mine)

There is joy in the Holy Ghost. Commence a serious relationship with the Holy Spirit and experience this joy. There is also peace that surpasses all understanding in the Holy Spirit. Some years ago, I made a sacrificial offering unto the Lord, and He responded by filling me up with internal and external peace and joy that passed all understanding which kept my heart and mind through my Lord Jesus Christ. It was a pleasant unforgettable encounter of the love, peace, and joy of the Lord. He also gave me a powerful word. That's how I had experiential knowledge of Philippians 4:7 and Romans 14:17. For about one month, peace, and joy became my food. I wasn't fasting yet I was rarely hungry. I call it invisible spiritual food from heaven, which to me is superior to visible manna. God gave me peace that passeth all understanding. Unexplainable peace! Praise God! That was the Holy Spirit demonstrating that He is happy with me, and showed me love.

*Romans 15:30*

*Now I beseech you, brethren, for the Lord Jesus Christ's sake, and for <u>the love of the Spirit,</u> that ye strive together with me in your prayers to God for me;* (Underline mine)

The above scripture also tells us there is love of the Spirit. The Holy Spirit is love. He loves people, and that makes Him a person. Connect to His love.

**WILL** – The Holy Spirit has a will to make His own decisions. This shows that He is a person.

## 7. The Holy Spirit has a will

*1 Corinthians 12:11*

*But all these worketh that one and the selfsame Spirit, dividing to every man severally as he will.*

With reference to the 9 gifts of the Spirit, we see that the Holy Spirit is responsible for assigning various gifts to different people as He will. He makes the decision who to give a gift of the Spirit, where and when to manifest them. No one tells Him what to do. This is the character of a person.

*Let's now look at more scriptures which demonstrates that the Holy Spirit is a person.*

## 8. The Holy Spirit speaks

The Holy Spirit speaks. This is another quality He demonstrates that makes Him a person.

*Acts 8:29*

*<u>Then the Spirit said unto Philip,</u> Go near, and join thyself to this chariot.* (Underline mine)

The above scripture clearly tells us that the Holy Spirit spoke to Philip before he went to minister to the Ethiopian eunuch. This means that the Holy Spirit speaks and knows a person who is ready to receive Jesus Christ and He will lead us to witness to the person. This is a very effective way of evangelism.

## Acts 10:19

*While Peter thought on the vision, <u>the Spirit said unto him</u>, Behold, three men seek thee.* (Underline mine)

In the above verse, we see the Holy Spirit speak to Peter to respond to the men Cornelius sent to him to come and minister to him. Peter went with them and while he preached to Cornelius and his household, the Holy Ghost fell on them and they all received salvation, filled with the Holy Spirit, and spoke in tongues. Peter recorded such a great success because the Holy Spirit directed him. This is a great way to evangelize.

## Acts 13:1-2

*[1] Now there were in the church that was at Antioch certain prophets and teachers; as Barnabas, and Simeon that was called Niger, and Lucius of Cyrene, and Manaen, which had been brought up with Herod the tetrarch, and Saul.*

*[2] As they ministered to the Lord, and fasted, <u>the Holy Ghost said</u>, Separate me Barnabas and Saul for the work whereunto I have called them.* (Underline mine)

The Holy Spirit spoke to certain prophets and teachers in the Antioch church as they fasted and ministered to the Lord. This should be a wakeup call to the modern day church and the body of Christ that as we desire for the Holy Spirit to speak we have to step up our spiritual exercise.

The Holy Spirit is both invisible and intangible, yet verse 2 above says *"the Holy Ghost said."* This seems to be a mystery, incredible, and amazing. But the truth is that if the Bible recorded that He spoke, then He did. However, the Bible did not say in what form He spoke, because He could have spoken in any other form apart from audibly.

## Acts 21:11

*And when he was come unto us, he took Paul's girdle, and bound his own hands and feet, and said, <u>Thus saith the Holy Ghost</u>, So shall the Jews at Jerusalem bind the man that owneth this girdle, and shall deliver him into the hands of the Gentiles.* (Underline mine)

This is another scenario where we see the Holy Ghost speaking. Powerful!

## Revelation 2:7

*He that hath an ear, let him hear <u>what the Spirit saith</u> unto the churches; To him that overcometh will I give to eat of the tree of life, which is in the midst of the paradise of God.* (Underline mine)

Is the Holy Spirit speaking? Yes! However, it is only those who have an ear that will hear Him. This is not necessarily only your physical visible natural ears, but also your spiritual invisible ear. The Holy Spirit interacts with our human spirit. It's only those who are paying attention that will hear. It's only those who desire and expect to hear that will hear. Only those who are discerning or perceiving will hear. It's only those who are in a peaceful environment that will hear. Those who are in a very noisy environment may not hear Him. Those who always have their ears plugged listening to ungodly music and messages from their mobile may not hear the Holy Spirit. But when you isolate yourself in a quiet atmosphere, you are likely to hear the Holy Spirit. The above five examples should challenge someone to be determined to hear from the Holy Spirit. Jesus said in:

*John 10:27*

*My sheep hear my voice, and I know them, and they follow me:*

As a believer, when you are *obedient* to biblical principles, you will hear Jesus speak to you as a shepherd speaks to his sheep.

Note that the Holy Spirit speaks in some other ways apart from audibly. For example, He can speak to your spirit, show a vision, dream, give you a word as you read your Bible, give you peace or withdraw your peace, give you a prophetic word through someone etc. Have an open mind and be ready to receive a word from Him from any genuine source it comes and not necessarily the way you are expecting it to come. Judge all the leading and word you receive with the Word of God. That's our umpire.

## 9. The Holy Spirit leads

*Romans 8:14*

*For as many as are led by the Spirit of God, they are the sons of God.*

The above scripture clearly tells us that the Holy Spirit leads. But does He lead everybody? No! In the kingdom of God, we have babies, sons, fathers, and generals. For the Holy Spirit to start leading you properly, you have to grow up and mature to be at least a son in the body of Christ. How can I achieve this? One of the ways you can achieve this is by studying your Bible more. *1 Peter 2:2* says *"As newborn babes, desire the sincere milk of the word, that ye may grow thereby:"* Feed yourself with more of the sword of the Spirit, which is the Word of God – Ephesians 6:17, and that will bring you in union with Him to lead you.

The great thing about the leading of the Holy Spirit is that He will lead you in everything you do no matter your profession, gender, or age. Remember that you also need to receive and believe in

Jesus Christ to become sons of God. *John 1:12* says *"But as many as received him, to them gave he power to become the sons of God, even to them that believe on his name:"* Grow and mature to become a son of God and the Holy Spirit will lead you.

Jesus said in:

## Matthew 15:14

*Let them alone: they be blind leaders of the blind. And if the blind lead the blind, both shall fall into the ditch.*

The blind cannot lead the blind otherwise they will both crash into the pit. The leading of the Holy Spirit is superior to the leading of men. Therefore, the Holy Spirit is indeed a person to be able to lead human beings.

## 10. The Holy Spirit can be resisted

*Acts 7:51*

*Ye stiffnecked and uncircumcised in heart and ears, <u>ye do always resist the Holy Ghost</u>: as your fathers did, so do ye.* (Underline mine)

Deacon Stephen, speaking to the council members in the Sanhedrin, called the high priests stiffnecked or stubborn, uncircumcised in heart and ears, always resisting the Holy Ghost. Whao! What a terrible state a person can find himself in. Always resisting God? Is this not pride? Avoid selfishness, ego, and pride because this can be a source of resistance to the Holy Spirit. Be humble!

If the Holy Spirit can be resisted, it shows He has the quality of a person. It is better not to resist the Holy Spirit from accomplishing what He wants to do in your life. Surrender to Him. He has better plans for you.

Note that those who resist the Holy Spirit through pride can face greater resistance. The Bible says in:

*James 4:6*

*But he giveth more grace. Wherefore he saith, God resisteth the proud, but giveth grace unto the humble.*

## 11. The Holy Spirit can be quenched

*1 Thessalonians 5:19 - Quench not the Spirit.*

Don't quench or allow others to quench the move of the Holy Spirit. If the Holy Spirit can be quenched, it shows He is a person. Always create the right atmosphere to enable the awesome fire of the Holy Spirit to keep burning, stirring, and flowing. Don't suppress or dampen the praise, worship, and fire of the Holy Spirit. Always keep up with your enthusiastic spiritual attitude. Don't let those who call you names like, "Fanatic", "Church boy or girl" dampen your spirit. *Hebrews 12:29* says, *"For our God is a consuming fire."* Let that fire burn and consume the works of the devil and every ungodly thing in Jesus' name. Amen!

*As we consider further the characteristics of the Holy Spirit that makes Him a person, I would like us to round it up by examining one scripture from the Amplified Classic Edition of the Bible.*

*John 14:26*

*But the Comforter (Counselor, Helper, Intercessor, Advocate, Strengthener, Standby), the Holy Spirit, Whom the Father will send in My name [in My place, to represent Me and act on My behalf], He will <u>teach</u> you all things. And He will cause you to recall (will <u>remind</u> you of, bring to your remembrance) everything I have told you. (Underline mine)*

From the above scripture, we can see that the Holy Spirit is our

- Comforter
- Counsellor
- Helper
- Intercessor
- Advocate
- Strengthener
- Standby
- Teacher
- Reminder

We will further consider the above nine characteristics of the Holy Spirit because they further confirm that He is a person. As I already mentioned in the Preface section of this book, the Holy Spirit is called *Parakletos*[6] in Greek because of the above nine features.

## 12. The Holy Spirit is our Comforter

The Holy Spirit indwells a believer to comfort him. Life would have been a lot more terrible without Him.

### 2 Corinthians 1:3-4

[3] *Blessed be God, even the Father of our Lord Jesus Christ, the Father of mercies, and the God of all comfort;*

[4] *Who comforteth us in all our tribulation, that we may be able to comfort them which are in any trouble, by the comfort wherewith we ourselves are comforted of God.*

### Psalms 71:21

*Thou shalt increase my greatness, and comfort me on every side.*

The Holy Spirit is God, and I have already mentioned that He is part of the Trinity – 3 persons in one God. We will discuss this further in the next chapter. Since the Holy Spirit is also God, He comforts us in tribulation as God. Since the Holy Spirit is our Comforter, then He is a person. My prayer for you is that the Holy Spirit will deliver you, and always comfort you on every side no matter the tribulation in Jesus' name.

## 13. The Holy Spirit is our Counsellor

The Holy Spirit dwells within a believer to interact with him when there is a relationship, not when He is grieved, ignored, and made dormant. It is the Holy Spirit speaking to you whenever you say, "Something told me or I just know…." That something is the Holy Spirit. The Holy Spirit manifests as that *"inward witness"*, or *"small still voice"* within you as a believer. That your *"intuition"* or *"hunch"* could also be an indication the Holy Spirit is speaking. Don't ignore Him. Always judge what you hear with the Word of God before you approve or discount the Holy Spirit. You will know He is the person speaking if what you perceive or hear agrees with the Word of God.

*Psalms 32:8*

*I will instruct thee and teach thee in the way which thou shalt go: I will guide thee with mine eye.*

It's important to follow the instruction, teaching, direction, and guidance of the Holy Spirit because strict adherence will guarantee your victory. To counsel also means to give advice. Ensure you follow biblical principles and patterns. They may appear foolish and senseless sometimes, but just follow Him. In John chapter 2, Jesus was at a wedding and their wine finished. He instructed the servants to fill six water pots with water and it turned to wine. How do you explain that? Is this not more than science and technology? Does that not appear to be a senseless instruction? Yet the servants *obeyed* and the desired result manifested. Best wine! The Holy Spirit knows more than us. He is the master planner and God. Whatever He says to you, just do it! – John 2:5.

*Proverbs 11:14*

*Where no counsel is, the people fall: but in the multitude of counsellors there is safety.*

How will you further know the Holy Spirit is the one counselling you? When you have peace and safety.

## 14. The Holy Spirit is our Helper

*Hebrews 13:5 (Amplified Classic Edition)*

Let your [a]*character or moral disposition be free from love of money [including greed, avarice, lust, and craving for earthly possessions] and be satisfied with your present [circumstances and with what you have]; for He [God]* [b]*Himself has said, I will not in any way fail you nor* [c]*give you up nor leave you without support.* [I will] not, [d][I will] not, [I will] not in any degree leave you helpless nor forsake nor [e]let [you] down ([f]relax My hold on you)! [g]Assuredly not!] (Underline mine)

God is indeed true to His Word. He said 3 times in the above scripture, "*I will not...leave you helpless...*" Whao! Trust Him 100%, and He will show up with excess help for you. One day, many years ago, I had no money and food, but I had this Word of God I just shared with you here. I read it again and again. Meditated on it, got excited and started laughing and dancing. It wasn't long before a gentleman I met for the first time showed up and blessed me with some money. God will send you help through unexpected channels so that you will marvel and praise Him more. I prophesy to you that help is on the way for you by the Holy Ghost in Jesus' name.

*Psalms 46:1*

*God is our refuge and strength, a very present help in trouble.* Receive the help of God now in Jesus' name. Amen!

*The Holy Spirit Intercedes for us. This has been discussed in number 2 point above.*

## 15. The Holy Spirit is our Advocate

*1 John 2:1*

*My little children, these things write I unto you, that ye sin not. And if any man sin, we have an advocate with the Father, Jesus Christ the righteous:*

An advocate is an associate who helps in times of need acting as a spokesperson. A barrister acting on behalf of his client is an example of an advocate. The Holy Spirit and our Lord Jesus Christ also act in such a capacity to defend us against the accuser, Satan. And when the Holy Spirit or Jesus stands for you, your victory is guaranteed. Jesus paid the highest substitutionary price of death on the cross of Calvary to save us from our sin. You've got to be a person to be an Advocate. The Holy Spirit is a person.

## 16. The Holy Spirit is our Strengthener

*Isaiah 40:29-31*

*29 He giveth power to the faint; and to them that have no might he increaseth strength.*

*30 Even the youths shall faint and be weary, and the young men shall utterly fall.*

*31 But they that wait upon the LORD shall renew their strength; they shall mount up with wings as eagles; they shall run, and not be weary; and they shall walk, and not faint.*

The Holy Spirit gives power to the faint, and increases the strength of those who have no might. Waiting upon the Lord will also renew a believer's strength and make him soar as an eagle. Connect to Holy Ghost power.

## 17. The Holy Spirit is our Standby

*Hebrews 13:5* says "*….He hath said, I will never leave thee, nor forsake thee.*" He says again in *Matthew 28:20*, "*… Lo, I am with* *you alway, even unto the end of the world. Amen."* And Psalms 91:11, says *"For he shall give his angels charge over thee, to keep thee in all thy ways."* No shaking! No fretting! No panicking! You always have a person standing by you. The Holy Spirit is a powerful Standby every moment to shield you in Jesus' name. Amen!

## 18. The Holy Spirit is our Teacher

*1 John 2:27*

*But the anointing which ye have received of him abideth in you, and ye need not that any man teach you: but as the same anointing teacheth you of all things, and is truth, and is no lie, and even as it hath taught you, ye shall abide in him.*

*1 John 2:20*

*But ye have an unction from the Holy One, and ye know all things.*

The anointing of the Holy Ghost within a believer is there to teach us all things. We are to humble ourselves, yield, and co-operate with the Holy Ghost to teach, and show us great and mighty things we know not. The Holy Spirit is a person for Him to be a teacher.

## 19. The Holy Spirit is our Reminder

Note that the Holy Spirit is to remind us *first*, those things Jesus said and taught us in the Word of God. And *second*, positive things that will edify us, empower us, give us hope, and be beneficial to us. We are not to remember negative unproductive things of the past. Trash them!

*Lamentations 3:21*

*This I recall to my mind, therefore have I hope.*

My prayer for you is that the Holy Spirit will continually remind you of scriptures, and other positive things that will help edify and empower you in life in Jesus' name. Amen!

## 20. The Holy Spirit is our Guide and shows us things to come

*John 16:13*

*Howbeit when he, the Spirit of truth, is come, he will guide you into all truth: for he shall not speak of himself; but whatsoever he shall hear, that shall he speak: and he will shew you things to come.*

What is it that you want to commence or currently undertaking and you are not making progress? Is it your ministry, career, business, marriage, projects, or academic pursuit? This is your opportunity to practice what you are learning in this book by inviting the most powerful person in the world called the Holy Spirit to help you. He will guide, direct, and lead you by giving you supernatural strategies. The Bible says in:

*Psalms 32:8*

*I will instruct thee and teach thee in the way which thou shalt go: I will guide thee with mine eye.*

Follow the instructions, teachings, and guidance of the Holy Spirit and you will safely and successfully arrive at your desired destination. It's important to note that even when the instruction appears to be foolish and senseless, you just have to hearken to the Holy Spirit. The Bible says in:

*Acts 16:6*

*Now when they had gone throughout Phrygia and the region of Galatia, and were forbidden of the Holy Ghost to preach the word in Asia,*

The Bible tells us in the above scripture that Apostle Paul and his missionary team were forbidden to preach the gospel in Asia. Does this make sense? It doesn't make sense because one of the main commandments Jesus gave to us is to preach the gospel. See Mark 16:15 and Matthew 28:19-20. Therefore, it appears to be a foolish thing for the Holy Ghost to stop Paul and his team from preaching in Asia. However, Paul obeyed the Holy Ghost and did not go. This is just one example of a kind of seemingly senseless instruction the Holy Ghost can give to a person.

Sometimes, this sort of instruction could turn out to be a test. It's your duty to make sure that you pass the test.

## Genesis 22:1-2

*¹ And it came to pass after these things, that <u>God did tempt Abraham</u>, and said unto him, Abraham: and he said, Behold, here I am.*

*² And he said, Take now thy son, thine only son Isaac, whom thou lovest, and get thee into the land of Moriah; and offer him there for a burnt offering upon one of the mountains which I will tell thee of.* (Underline mine)

Why on earth will God ask Abraham to take his only son Isaac that he loves and offer him as a sacrifice? Does it make sense? No! Does it not appear to be a foolish instruction? Of course it does appear to be a foolish instruction. Why should a human being be offered for a sacrifice? The child you had at the age of 100 years that you love. This sort of instruction will cause a man to wonder if it was truly the voice of God he heard and not the devil. Well, it all turned out to be a test after Abraham obeyed.

## Isaiah 30:21

*And thine ears shall hear a word behind thee, saying, This is the way, walk ye in it, when ye turn to the right hand, and when ye turn to the left.*

Note that the Holy Spirit can speak to you audibly, guiding and directing you with strategies you need to accomplish a project, business, or an assignment. Just desire and expect Him to speak and guide you, and He will in Jesus' name. Amen!

## 21. The Holy Spirit convicts

*John 16:8*

*And when he is come, he will reprove the world of sin, and of righteousness, and of judgment:*

The Word of God combined with the power of the Holy Spirit is a very effective tool for evangelism. The Word of God reproves people with stony hearts, so called atheists, and agnostics of sin, righteousness, and judgment.

*Acts 2:37*

*Now when they heard this, <u>they were pricked in their heart</u>, and said unto Peter and to the rest of the apostles, Men and brethren, what shall we do?* (Underline is mine)

On the day of Pentecost, and shortly after the baptism of the Holy Ghost, Apostle Peter preached. As he preached, the Word of God which is also the sword of the Spirit, quick and powerful, sharper than any two edged sword, pierced through and pricked their heart. The Holy Spirit reproves. About 3 thousand people gave their life to Jesus that day and were baptised – Acts 2:41.

For three thousand people to give their life to Jesus in one go as at then shows the awesome power of the Holy Spirit in evangelism. Acts 4:4 tells us that a further five thousand people believed and that increased the number to eight thousand. Glory!

There has been a repeat of similar subsequent moves of the Holy Ghost in revivals such as the Azusa street revival in Los Angeles,

California led by Pastor William Seymour from about 1906 to about 1915. The great Revivalist Evan Roberts also led the remarkable Welsh revival from about 1904 to 1905 through the power of the Holy Spirit. Many people gave their life to Jesus. Glory be to God!

The great Evangelists Charles Finney, John Wesley, D L Moody, Billy Graham, Oral Roberts, and Reinhard Bonnke all accomplished great success in their ministry through the power of the Holy Ghost.

In 2016, I was in Pakistan where I preached in a crusade. I saw the powerful move of the Holy Spirit to convict, deliver, and heal the people of God. Notable signs, wonders, and miracles happened through the power of the Holy Spirit. The Holy Spirit is the supernatural agent we need for effective evangelism. Glory be to God!

I pray and believe that there will be much greater moves of the power of the Holy Ghost in our generation because the glory of the latter shall be more than the former. Hallelujah!

## Acts 24:24-25

*24 And after certain days, when Felix came with his wife Drusilla, which was a Jewess, he sent for Paul, and heard him concerning the faith in Christ.*

*25 And as he reasoned of righteousness, temperance, and judgment to come, <u>Felix trembled</u>, and answered, Go thy way for this time; when I have a convenient season, I will call for thee.* (Underline mine)

The above scripture tells us that Governor Felix trembled when Paul started declaring the Word of God. That was the Holy Spirit convicting Governor Felix. Powerful!

*Acts 26:28*

*Then Agrippa said unto Paul, Almost thou persuadest me to be a Christian.*

Apostle Paul was brought before Governor Festus and King Agrippa, and as he declared the Word of God, King Agrippa confessed to Paul that he almost convinced him to become a Christian. That was the power of the Holy Spirit convicting King Agrippa as Paul preached. My prayer is that the Holy Spirit will continually convict people of sin, righteousness, and judgment to be born again by touching all stony hearts to become a heart of flesh filled with the Holy Spirit and the power of God in Jesus' name. Amen!

## CONCLUSION

We are in the era and dispensation of the Holy Spirit. Believers, the church, and the body of Christ needs to raise awareness of this fact by teaching, proclaiming, and embracing the consciousness of the Holy Spirit in all that we do. Jesus said in *John 15:5, "... For without me ye can do nothing."* Now that Jesus is gone to be with the Father, and sent us the Holy Spirit, I think it is safe to also say the same thing about the Holy Spirit since He is part of the Trinity. Without the Holy Spirit, we can do nothing meaningful. Therefore, trust and depend on Him in all you do, and you will triumph.

For the Holy Spirit to operate in the above 21 dimensions we have discussed surely proves that the Holy Spirit is indeed a person. Be conscious of Him. He is real, and closer to you than you imagine. He is your Friend!

**NOTE:** I want to make a very important point here. I divided this subject of the Holy Spirit into three chapters as follows: The Holy Spirit is a person; the Holy Spirit is God; and the Names and Works of the Holy Spirit. However, there may not be a clear cut distinction with some points I have discussed because they can effectively be applied to not just a particular chapter, but to two or even all three chapters. For example, John 14:26 of the Amplified Classic Bible I discussed above featured 9 points about the Holy Spirit and some of them can be used to describe Him as a person, as well as His function and ministry.

Who you are, and what you do as a person may sometimes be hard to separate. This means that the functions of the Holy Spirit as a ministry, or His features as a person can sometimes be *interwoven* with reference to some scriptures. Hopefully this statement should clear the argument that this point or that point should not be in this chapter or that chapter. I have tried my best with the help of the Holy Spirit to distinguish the points. One of the approaches I adopted is to underline certain parts of the scriptures I used for clarity purposes. I hope this explanation helps.

# CHAPTER TWO

# THE HOLY SPIRIT IS GOD

## DIVINE ATTRIBUTES OF THE HOLY SPIRIT

The Holy Spirit is God. As mentioned in Chapter one, we will examine some of the characteristics of the Holy Spirit that makes Him God.

### 1. The Holy Spirit is Omnipotent

Omnipotent means all powerful. The Holy Spirit is part of the Trinity. The Holy Spirit is so powerful that He can do and undo things. He had to manifest from Genesis during creation, and also in the life of Jesus Christ from conception, baptism in the Holy Spirit, and resurrection.

*Genesis 1:1-2*

*[1] In the beginning God created the heaven and the earth.*

*[2] And the earth was without form, and void; and darkness was upon the face of the deep. And the Spirit of God moved upon the face of the waters.* – The Holy Spirit action in the creation.

*Luke 1:35*

*And the angel answered and said unto her, The Holy Ghost shall come upon thee, and the power of the Highest shall overshadow thee: therefore also that holy thing which shall be born of thee shall be called the Son of God.* – The Holy Spirit action in the conception of Jesus Christ.

*Romans 8:11*

*But if the Spirit of him that raised up Jesus from the dead dwell in you, he that raised up Christ from the dead shall also quicken your mortal bodies by his Spirit that dwelleth in you.* – The Holy Spirit action in the resurrection of Jesus Christ.

The Holy Spirit must be God or divine for Him to be able to perform the above functions. Powerful!

## 2. The Holy Spirit is Omnipresent

The Holy Spirit is invisible, intangible, and He is present everywhere at the same time just like God. Our Lord Jesus Christ did not have this ability of being everywhere at the same time when He walked on earth. It is part of the reason why Jesus Himself said it is expedient that I go and send you the Holy Spirit. Read what King David said about the presence of the Holy Spirit in:

*Psalms 139:7-8*

*⁷ Whither shall I go from thy <u>spirit</u>?*
*or whither shall I flee from thy presence?*

*⁸ If I ascend up into heaven, thou art there:*
*if I make my bed in hell, behold, thou art there.* (Underline mine)

Note that the above underlined "spirit" in (KJV) should have been "Spirit" with capital letter 'S'. AMPC, NKJV, NAS, NIV etc all got it down as "Spirit". Therefore, King David was talking about the Holy Spirit, and not the human spirit or evil spirit as the underlined spirit suggests in the verse 7 text.

You can see from the above scripture penned down by King David that there is no hiding place from the Holy Spirit when there is an issue with anyone. Go to heaven, He is there. Go to hell, He is there. Oh Boy, don't play hide and seek with the Holy Spirit because He will definitely catch you. The Holy Spirit must be God or divine for Him to be everywhere at the same time.

### 3. The Holy Spirit is Omniscient

The Holy Spirit knows all things, even the deep things of God.

*1 Corinthians 2:10-11*

*[10] But God hath revealed them unto us by his Spirit: for the Spirit searcheth all things, yea, the deep things of God.*

*[11] For what man knoweth the things of a man, save the spirit of man which is in him? even so the things of God knoweth no man, but the Spirit of God.*

The Holy Spirit must be God or divine for Him to be able to perform the above function to know all things.

### 4. The Holy Spirit is eternal

*Hebrews 9:14*

*How much more shall the blood of Christ, who through the eternal Spirit offered himself without spot to God, purge your conscience from dead works to serve the living God?*

To be eternal also means to be everlasting. The Holy Spirit must be God or divine for Him to be able to perform the above eternal function.

### 5. The Holy Spirit is God

*Acts 5:3-4*

*[3] But Peter said, Ananias, why hath Satan filled thine heart to <u>lie to the Holy Ghost</u>, and to keep back part of the price of the land?*

⁴ *Whilst it remained, was it not thine own? and after it was sold, was it not in thine own power? why hast thou conceived this thing in thine heart? <u>thou hast not lied unto men, but unto God.</u>* (Underline mine)

In the above scripture, in verse 3, Apostle Peter asked Ananias why Satan got him to lie to the Holy Ghost. He told him in verse 4, "…. *thou hast not lied unto men, but unto God.*" This statement by Apostle Peter shows that the Holy Ghost and God are the same.

## 6. The Holy Spirit shares the same name with the Father and Son

*Matthew 28:18-20*

¹⁸ *And Jesus came and spake unto them, saying, All power is given unto me in heaven and in earth.*

¹⁹ *Go ye therefore, and teach all nations, baptizing them in the name of the Father, and of the Son, and of the Holy Ghost:*

²⁰ *Teaching them to observe all things whatsoever I have commanded you: and, lo, I am with you alway, even unto the end of the world. Amen.*

Verse 19 above is my point of emphasis. Jesus told the disciples to teach, and baptise in the name of the Father, and of the Son, and the Holy Ghost – Trinity. One God, three persons. This function puts the Holy Spirit in the same position of deity as the Father, and Son – He is God.

## 7. The Holy Spirit resurrects

*Romans 8:11*

*But if the Spirit of him that raised up Jesus from the dead dwell in you, he that raised up Christ from the dead shall also quicken your mortal bodies by his Spirit that dwelleth in you.*

The above verse tells us the Holy Spirit raised up Jesus Christ from the dead. Powerful! The Holy Spirit must be God with divine nature and capacity to be able to resurrect Jesus Christ.

## 8. The Holy Spirit empowers

*Acts 10:38*

*How God anointed Jesus of Nazareth with the Holy Ghost and with power: who went about doing good, and healing all that were oppressed of the devil; for God was with him.*

The above scripture tells us that God anointed Jesus with the Holy Ghost and with power. That's empowerment. For the Holy Spirit to function in this capacity to empower Jesus, another member of the Trinity shows He must be God.

## 9. The Holy Spirit is Holy

God is holy, and the Holy Spirit is also holy. This holiness puts both members of the Trinity in the same position as God. Jesus is also holy. We Christians are to be holy as well.

*1 Peter 1:16*

*Because it is written, Be ye holy; for I am holy.*

## 10. The Holy Spirit can be blasphemed

*Matthew 12:31-32*

*³¹ Wherefore I say unto you, All manner of sin and blasphemy shall be forgiven unto men: <u>but the blasphemy against the Holy Ghost shall not be forgiven unto men.</u>*

*³² And whosoever speaketh a word against the Son of man, it shall be forgiven him: but whosoever speaketh against the Holy Ghost, it shall not be forgiven him, neither in this world, neither in the world to come.* (Underline mine)

The above scripture says the Holy Spirit can be blasphemed. Therefore, if the Holy Spirit can be blasphemed, just like God, then He must be God. A word of caution: The underlined above in verse 31 says, "... *but the blasphemy against the Holy Ghost shall not be forgiven unto men...*" Beware not to blaspheme, desecrate, or profane the Holy Spirit because the sin will never be forgiven. To this, I say the Holy Spirit must be untouchable when it comes to blasphemy. Beware of the Holy Ghost Zone – Keep off from blasphemy.

## Psalms 14:1

*The fool hath said in his heart, There is no God. They are corrupt, they have done abominable works, there is none that doeth good.* (Underline mine)

Only foolish so called atheists say in their heart or audibly that there is no God. It's better not to join them blasphemously. The Holy Spirit knows your thoughts and hears even your whispers.

## CONCLUSION

As I mentioned earlier, we are in the era and dispensation of the Holy Spirit. Believers, the church, and the body of Christ need to raise awareness of this fact by teaching, proclaiming, and embracing the consciousness of the Holy Spirit in all that we do. God said in:

## Zechariah 4:6

"... *Not by might, nor by power, but by my spirit, saith the LORD of hosts.*" (Underline mine)

Note that the above underlined "spirit" should have been "Spirit" because the spirit is of God, which is the Holy Spirit. It is not human spirit or evil spirit. AMPC, NKJV, NAS, NIV etc put it down as "Spirit". See below how the New International Version (NIV) puts it.

## Zechariah 4:6

"…. 'Not by might nor by power, but by my <u>Spirit</u>,' says the LORD Almighty." *(NIV)* (Underline mine)

Even God acknowledged the Holy Spirit as His in the above verse saying, "… *but by my Spirit*…" For the Holy Spirit to manifest in the above 10 ways we discussed surely proves that the Holy Spirit is indeed of God, and God. Make no mistake about this. Treat Him exactly the same way you will treat God. Be conscious of Him. He is real, and closer to you than you imagine. He is your Friend!

# CHAPTER THREE

# THE NAMES AND WORKS OF THE HOLY SPIRIT

We will proceed further in this chapter to discuss various other kinds of Spirits. There are many of them. However, I will briefly discuss some of them. The ministry or function of the Holy Spirit is vast. For a more detailed study, you can consult your concordance and other study materials if you so desire.

*Isaiah 11:2*

*And the <u>spirit</u> of the LORD shall rest upon him,
the <u>spirit</u> of wisdom and understanding,
the <u>spirit</u> of counsel and might,
the <u>spirit</u> of knowledge and of the fear of the LORD;* (Underline mine)

*Isaiah 11:2 (NIV)*

*The Spirit of the LORD will rest on him—*

*the Spirit of wisdom and of understanding,
the Spirit of counsel and of might,
the Spirit of the knowledge and fear of the LORD—*

Four types of Spirits are mentioned in the above scripture. I had to underline the (KJV) "spirit" to highlight the fact that it should have been "Spirit", because the Spirit is of God, the Holy Spirit, and not human spirit or evil spirit. AMPC, NKJV, NAS, NIV etc all put it down as "Spirit." See above how the New International Version (NIV) stated it.

I would like to also draw your attention at this point about the way the word *LORD, Lord, and lord,* is used in the Bible in relation to Spirit.

LORD refers to Almighty God – Isaiah 11:2 above Spirit relates to LORD or God

Lord refers to Jesus Christ – 2 Corinthians 3:17 Spirit relates to Jesus Christ

lord refers to human lord, like a king or Master – Matthew 25:21 lord

It's important as you read your Bible to pay attention to the usage of *LORD* and *Lord* because they are *sometimes interchanged* depending on the verse and translation. For illustration purpose see:

## *Isaiah 4:2*

*In that day shall the branch of the <u>LORD</u> be beautiful and glorious,*
*and the fruit of the earth shall be excellent and comely*
*for them that are escaped of Israel.* (Underline mine)

## *Isaiah 4:2 (Amplified Classic Edition)*

*In that day the Branch of the <u>Lord</u> shall be beautiful and glorious, and the fruit of the land shall be excellent and lovely to those of Israel who have escaped.* (Underline mine)

Can you see that in the above scripture, Isaiah 4:2 (KJV) is (LORD), but in Amplified Classic Edition, it is (Lord). They are sometimes used interchangeably depending on verse and translation. Therefore, you need to pay close attention to such things. Let us now discuss the above Spirits.

## 1. The Spirit of the LORD

The Spirit of the LORD or God is supernatural, and relates to the Holy Spirit resting *upon* a person like we discussed in the Old Testament to carry out a special task, or someone in the position of a king, prophet, judge, or priest. We also know that because the Spirit comes *upon* the person, He can come and go. However, in the New Testament the Spirit is *indwelling* in a born again Christian. He abides in a Christian, but can be grieved, vexed, ignored, or made dormant.

For better result, a Christian needs to have a recreated or regenerated human spirit, with indwelling Holy Spirit, filled with the Holy Spirit or baptism of the Holy Spirit, and then fortified with the Power of the Holy Spirit to start doing exploits for the kingdom of God or whatever field God assigns and approves for them to operate in. This was the kind of Spirit that rested upon Jesus. Jesus said in:

*Luke 4:18-19*

*[18] The Spirit of the Lord is upon me, because he hath anointed me to preach the gospel to the poor; he hath sent me to heal the brokenhearted, to preach deliverance to the captives, and recovering of sight to the blind, to set at liberty them that are bruised,* (Underline mine)

*[19] To preach the acceptable year of the Lord.*

*Acts 10:38*

*How God anointed Jesus of Nazareth with the Holy Ghost and with power: who went about doing good, and healing all that were oppressed of the devil; for God was with him.*

While we are discussing the Spirit of the LORD, I would like to draw your attention to the fact that we have *positive* "Spirit of the LORD, and *negative* "spirit of the LORD." It's important that you pay a very close attention to how both are used in different verses and translations. There is something I said before in the Preface and Chapter one which I would like to repeat here because I really want you to get it. Please refer back to what I said about the scripture below in the Preface, and Chapter one of this book.

## 1 Samuel 16:14

*But the <u>Spirit of the LORD</u> departed from Saul, and an <u>evil spirit from the LORD</u> troubled him.* (Underline mine)

Let's look at one more example similar to the above scripture to clarify this point.

## 1 Kings 22:23

*Now therefore, behold, <u>the LORD hath put a lying spirit</u> in the mouth of all these thy prophets, and the LORD hath spoken evil concerning thee.* (Underline mine)

In the above scripture, is the underlined "*...the LORD hath put a lying spirit...*" correct usage? Yes! AMPC, NKJV, NAS, NIV etc all put it down as "spirit" just like (KJV). The spirit is *negative* lying spirit even though it is from the LORD. It is not *positive* Holy Spirit from the LORD. That's why it's correct with small letter spirit 's'.

*You can see from the above two examples that the Holy Spirit, evil spirit, and lying spirit proceeded from the LORD or God. Spirit or spirit differentiates them.*

## 2 Corinthians 3:18

*But we all, with open face beholding as in a glass the glory of the Lord, are changed into the same image from glory to glory, even as by the <u>Spirit of the Lord</u>.* (Underline mine)

As you can see from the above scripture, the Holy Spirit is our main agent of transformation. We are changed into the same image from glory to glory to be like Christ when the Holy Spirit imparts us. Therefore, we are to keep feeding ourselves with the sword of the Spirit which the Holy Spirit uses to renew us as we evolve into a better version of us. No metamorphosis, no profound glory.

## 2. The Spirit of wisdom and understanding

The Spirit of wisdom and understanding is imparted on a person by the Holy Spirit to accomplish a certain special task, or on a person occupying a godly office like king, prophet, judge, or priest. Examples are:

### Bezaleel

*Exodus 31:1-3*

*¹ And the LORD spake unto Moses, saying,*

*² See, I have called by name <u>Bezaleel</u> the son of Uri, the son of Hur, of the tribe of Judah:*

*³ <u>And I have filled him with the spirit of God, in wisdom, and in understanding</u>, and in knowledge, and in all manner of workmanship,* (Underline mine)

I have already explained in Chapter one that the above underlined "spirit of God" should have been "Spirit of God", because it relates to the Holy Spirit. Note that Bezaleel was able to commence and finish all the artistic cunning work in the sanctuary of the Lord according to the pattern prescribed by God because he was filled with the Holy Spirit. That's exactly what the Holy Spirit will do for you when He fills you up continuously, and you commune with Him intimately.

## Joshua

*Deuteronomy 34:9*

*And <u>Joshua</u> the son of Nun was full of the <u>spirit of wisdom</u>; for Moses had laid his hands upon him: and the children of Israel hearkened unto him, and did as the LORD commanded Moses.* (Underline mine)

The above underlined *"spirit of wisdom"* is written with small letter 's' for "spirit." This suggests that the spirit is not the Holy Spirit but Moses' human spirit that was transferred to Joshua. I checked other translations – AMPC, NKJV, NAS, NIV and they all got it down as *"spirit of wisdom."*

Moses laid hands on Joshua, and the spirit of wisdom was transferred to him. This is called spiritual impartation. A higher anointed vessel, ordained, wise servant of God can impart and empower his subordinates for special assignment. The Bible says in: *Hebrews 7:7, "And without all contradiction the less is blessed of the better."* I believe this impartation of wisdom from Moses to Joshua enabled him to successfully lead the Israelites into the Promised Land.

## Solomon

*1 Kings 3:12*

*Behold, I have done according to thy words: <u>lo, I have given thee a wise and an understanding heart</u>; so that there was none like thee before thee, neither after thee shall any arise like unto thee.* (Underline mine)

God said to King Solomon in the above scripture that He has given him a wise and understanding heart. From *Zechariah 4:6*, we know that God said, *"… Not by might, nor by power, but by my spirit, saith the LORD of hosts."* As I explained earlier, this Spirit is the Holy Spirit, and He is of God – *"by my Spirit"*.

We saw earlier that Bezaleel was also filled with the Spirit of wisdom by God. The Holy Spirit imparts wisdom. The Bible says in:

## James 1:5

*If any of you lack wisdom, let him ask of God, that giveth to all men liberally, and upbraideth not; and it shall be given him.*

You can ask God for wisdom as the above verse states. That's what King Solomon did. However, he went the extra mile by loving God and sacrificed a thousand burnt offerings to Him in 1 Kings 3:3-5. It appears this action by King Solomon helped to trigger God's response to give him a wise and an understanding heart.

## PRAYER FOR YOU

*Ephesians 1:16-18 (Amplified Classic Edition)*

[16] *I do not cease to give thanks for you, making mention of you in my prayers.*

[17] *[For I always pray to] the God of our Lord Jesus Christ, the Father of glory, that He may grant you a spirit of wisdom and revelation [of insight into mysteries and secrets] in the [deep and intimate] knowledge of Him,*

[18] *By having the eyes of your heart flooded with light, so that you can know and understand the hope to which He has called you, and how rich is His glorious inheritance in the saints (His set-apart ones),* in Jesus' name. Amen!

## 3. The Spirit of counsel and might

The Holy Spirit counsels and strengthens us. John 14:16 of the Amplified Classic Edition we looked at earlier tells us that He is our Counsellor. See point 13 of Chapter one.

*Ephesians 3:16*

*That he would grant you, according to the riches of his glory, <u>to be strengthened with might by his Spirit</u> in the inner man;* (Underline mine)

Joseph and Daniel were blessed with the gift of interpretation of dreams and counsel and this made them excel in Egypt and Babylon respectively.

## Joseph

After Joseph interpreted Pharaoh's dreams, and counselled him on what to do, read what Pharaoh said in:

*Genesis 41:38*

*And Pharaoh said unto his servants, Can we find such a one as this is, <u>a man in whom the Spirit of God is?</u>* (Underline mine)

Pharaoh made Joseph the Prime Minister of Egypt, in charge of the administrative, and economic affairs of the nation.

## Daniel

After Daniel also interpreted King Nebuchadnezzar's dream and counselled him, read what King Nebuchadnezzar said and did in:

*Daniel 2:47-48*

*[47] The king answered unto Daniel, and said, Of a truth it is, that your God is a God of gods, and a Lord of kings, and a revealer of secrets, seeing thou couldest reveal this secret.*

*[48] Then the king made Daniel a great man, and gave him many great gifts, and made him ruler over the whole province of Babylon, and chief of the governors over all the wise men of Babylon.*

Daniel's wisdom, and excellence dazzled and marvelled King Nebuchadnezzar so much that he said and did what you just read in the above scripture.

## Daniel 6:3

*Then this <u>Daniel</u> was preferred above the presidents and princes, because an <u>excellent spirit was in him</u>; and the king thought to set him over the whole realm.* (Underline mine)

Daniel had an excellent spirit and this helped him to serve as a President in the governments of Kings Nebuchadnezzar, Belshazzar, Darius, and Cyrus. Great Man of God, and politician.

## Samson

## Judges 14:6

*<u>And the Spirit of the LORD came mightily upon him</u>, and he rent him as he would have rent a kid, and he had nothing in his hand: but he told not his father or his mother what he had done.*

Samson was a man of power, strength, and might. On this occasion, he killed a lion with his bare hands.

## 4. The Spirit of knowledge and of the fear of the LORD

## Ephesians 1:17

*[17] That the God of our Lord Jesus Christ, the Father of glory, may give unto you the <u>spirit of wisdom and revelation in the knowledge of him:</u>* (Underline mine)

## Ephesians 1:17 (NIV)

*I keep asking that the God of our Lord Jesus Christ, the glorious Father, may give you the <u>Spirit</u>[a] <u>of wisdom and revelation, so that you may know him better</u>.* (Underline mine)

In the underlined scriptures above, I have laid Ephesians 1:17 of the KJV and NIV side by side above just for you to see that the KJV put down "spirit" with small letter 's' which does not appear to be right because the spirit is of God. However, NIV got it right by putting it down as "Spirit" because the Spirit is the Holy Spirit of God.

The Holy Spirit imparts wisdom, revelation, and knowledge to believers. That is what the Apostle Paul prayed for believers here. I pray the same for you.

*Psalms 111:10*

*The fear of the LORD is the beginning of wisdom: a good understanding have all they that do his commandments: his praise endureth for ever.*

Note that the fear of God in the above scripture is not one that you will start being scared, nervous, and hiding from God because He will bully you, or smack you. No! It's talking about reverential fear or respect for God. So relax and be calm. When you truly fear God as the above scripture says, you will do your Bible study, and be *obedient* to His Word. You will honor God, and put Him first in all you do in life. You will enthrone Him, and surrender all to Him.

## 5. The Spirit of truth

*John 16:13*

*Howbeit when he, <u>the Spirit of truth</u>, is come, he will guide you into all truth: for he shall not speak of himself; but whatsoever he shall hear, that shall he speak: and he will shew you things to come.* (Underline mine)

*John 14:17*

*Even <u>the Spirit of truth</u>; whom the world cannot receive, because it seeth him not, neither knoweth him: but ye know him; for he dwelleth with you, and shall be in you.* (Underline mine)

The Holy Spirit imparts truth to believers through communion and interaction with the sword of the Spirit. Feed yourself with the Word of God regularly. Jesus says in *John 6:63*, *"It is the spirit that quickeneth; the flesh profiteth nothing: the words that I speak unto you, they are spirit, and they are life."* He says again in, *John 8:32*, *"And ye shall know the truth, and the truth shall make you free."* Logically, if the truth makes people free, then lies will keep them in bondage. Forsake all lies now, and be free indeed. Lies belong to the devil.

## 6. The sword of the Spirit

*Ephesians 6:17*

*And take the helmet of salvation, and <u>the sword of the Spirit, which is the word of God:</u>* (Underline mine)

The Holy Spirit does not work alone or in isolation of the sword of the Spirit which is the Word of God. Eat the Word of God.

*Jeremiah 15:16*

*<u>Thy words were found, and I did eat them</u>; and thy word was unto me the joy and rejoicing of mine heart: for I am called by thy name, O LORD God of hosts.* (Underline mine)

The Word of God is the raw material the Holy Spirit uses to work effectively to impart a believer.

*Psalms 119:130*

*The entrance of thy words giveth light; it giveth understanding unto the simple.*

The logos or Word of God you eat, meditate on through the power of the Holy Spirit will give you light, illuminate you, and produce revelation and Rhema word. Eat the Word of God!

## 7. The Spirit of Christ

*Romans 8:9*

*But ye are not in the flesh, but in the Spirit, if so be that the Spirit of God dwell in you. Now if any man have not the <u>Spirit of Christ</u>, he is none of his.* (Underline mine)

People who believe and have confessed that Jesus Christ is their Lord and Savior, with regenerated spirit are considered to have the Spirit of Christ and are called Christians. The Spirit of Christ in a believer imparts life, "*...Christ in me the hope of glory.*" "*....Christ liveth in me...*" Read what the scripture below says about having Jesus.

*1 John 5:12*

*He that hath the Son hath life; and he that hath not the Son of God hath not life.*

## 8. The Spirit of God

The Spirit of God indwells a born again Christian. God dwelt in the built temples and tabernacles, and the ark of the covenant of the Lord in the holy of holies in the Old Testament. The people who had the Holy Spirit had it *upon* them which means He can come and go. But in the New Testament, our body became the temple of the Holy Spirit to dwell in.

*1 Corinthians 3:16*

*Know ye not that ye are the temple of God, and that <u>the Spirit of God dwelleth in you</u>?* (Underline mine)

*Romans 8:9*

*But ye are not in the flesh, but in the Spirit, if so be that <u>the Spirit of God</u> dwell in you. Now if any man have not the Spirit of Christ, he is none of his.* (Underline mine)

## Joseph

*Genesis 41:38*

*And Pharaoh said unto his servants, Can we find such a one as this is, <u>a man in whom the Spirit of God is</u>?* (Underline mine)

The above scripture tells us that Joseph had the Spirit of God in him. No wonder he became a great Man of God, and Prime Minister in a foreign land, Egypt as a slave and prisoner.

## 9. The Spirit of holiness

*Romans 1:4*

*And declared to be the Son of God with power, according to the <u>spirit of holiness</u>, by the resurrection from the dead:* (Underline mine)

Note that the above underlined *"spirit of holiness"* should have been *"Spirit of holiness"* because the Spirit is of God. AMPC, NKJV, NAS, NIV etc all put it down as *"Spirit of holiness."* See below how (NIV) put it:

*Romans 1:4 (NIV)*

*and who through the <u>Spirit of holiness</u> was appointed the Son of God in power[b] by his resurrection from the dead: Jesus Christ our Lord.* (Underline mine)

We have already seen in Chapter two that the Holy Spirit and other members of the Trinity are holy. The consecration of the Holy Spirit is so tremendous that He raised Jesus from the dead. Purity and holiness is essential to enable revival and restoration to happen. The Holy Spirit is a powerful agent of holiness. Let Him impart you by yielding and co-operating with Him.

## 10. The Spirit of life

*Romans 8:2*

*For the law of the <u>Spirit of life</u> in Christ Jesus hath made me free from the law of sin and death.* (Underline mine)

Jesus died on the cross as a substitute for our sin. This means we are forgiven. When we become born again with a regenerated spirit, we receive the Spirit of life in Christ. And the Holy Spirit begins to also impart us.

*2 Corinthians 5:17*

*Therefore if any man be in Christ, he is a new creature: old things are passed away; behold, all things are become new.*

## 11. The Spirit of grace

Grace is an unmerited favor of God. Grace means *Charis* in Greek. We see this grace in operation in the salvation of a believer.

*Ephesians 2:8*

*<u>For by grace are ye saved</u> through faith; and that not of yourselves: it is the gift of God:* (Underline mine)

This grace is imparted to us by the Holy Spirit.

*Hebrews 10:29*

*Of how much sorer punishment, suppose ye, shall he be thought worthy, who hath trodden under foot the Son of God, and hath counted the blood of the covenant, wherewith he was sanctified, an unholy thing, and hath done despite unto the <u>Spirit of grace</u>?* (Underline mine)

The Holy Spirit of grace enables us to do great and mighty things. The grace of God produces miracles in our lives.

## 1 Corinthians 15:9-10

*⁹ For I am the least of the apostles, that am not meet to be called an apostle, because I persecuted the church of God.*

*¹⁰ But by the <u>grace</u> of God I am what I am: and his <u>grace</u> which was bestowed upon me was not in vain; but I laboured more abundantly than they all: yet not I, but the <u>grace</u> of God which was with me.* (Underline mine)

Apostle Paul admitted in the above scripture that he was not even fit to be an apostle because he persecuted the church of God. But by the grace of God, he became an apostle and labored so much – Author of about two third of the epistles in the New Testament. He wrote some of them like Philippians while in chains in the prison. Whao! That's labor indeed. But let's thank God for His grace as well. Read 1 Corinthians 11:23-27 and see a catalogue of the things he suffered. Crushing experiences! Satan attacked and buffeted him with a thorn in the flesh. He cried out to Jesus for help, and Jesus said to him in *2 Corinthians 12:9,"...My grace is sufficient for thee: for my strength is made perfect in weakness..."*

Apostle Paul said the grace bestowed upon me was not in vain. I used it to write epistles, preach the gospel, set up churches etc. We need to start making use of the grace God bestowed upon us to do great things and stop making excuses.

## Romans 5:20

*Moreover the law entered, that the offence might abound. But where sin abounded, grace did much more abound:*

## Romans 6:1-2

*¹ What shall we say then? Shall we continue in sin, that grace may abound?*

*² God forbid. How shall we, that are dead to sin, live any longer therein?*

*Romans 6:14*

*For sin shall not have dominion over you: for ye are not under the law, but under grace.*

For some people, they see grace as a licence to act anyhow. They use grace as an excuse to commit all manner of blunders and sin but it shouldn't be so. Discipline yourself! My Friend, grace is an enabler because the Holy Spirit empowers you with grace.

## 12. Love in the Spirit

Man is a spirit, has a soul, and lives in a body. The Bible says in:

*Galatians 5:25*

*If we live in the Spirit, let us also walk in the Spirit.* (Underline mine)

To live in the Spirit, and walk in the Spirit simply means we have to be fully conscious of the fact that we are principally spiritual beings, and therefore have to continually sharpen our spirit with the sword of the Spirit (The Word of God - Ephesians 6:17) and other spiritual exercises. To live in the Spirit also means we need to have the mind of Christ, meditating on the Word of God. This will help the Holy Spirit interact well with our human spirit.

*Revelation 1:10*

*I was in the Spirit on the Lord's day, and heard behind me a great voice, as of a trumpet,* (Underline mine)

In the above scripture, the great Apostle of love, John said, "*I was in the Spirit...*" It takes walking in love to be in the Spirit. Where are you now? Are you in the Spirit or in the flesh? We've all got to be in the Spirit and not in the flesh in order to be overcomers and more than conquerors in life.

## Romans 8:9

*But ye are not in the flesh, but in the Spirit, if so be that the Spirit of God dwell in you. Now if any man have not the Spirit of Christ, he is none of his.* (Underline mine)

A man who operates in the Spirit can be invisible. He can appear in a place and vanish. Evangelist Phillip operated in that dimension. *First*, an angel spoke to him to go to Gaza. *Second*, the Spirit asked him to join the Ethiopian eunuch. Now read how he disappeared from Gaza to Azotus in:

## Acts 8:39-40

*[39] And when they were come up out of the water, the Spirit of the Lord caught away Philip, that the eunuch saw him no more: and he went on his way rejoicing.*

*[40] But Philip was found at Azotus: and passing through he preached in all the cities, till he came to Caesarea.* (Underline mine)

The Bible says again in:

## Galatians 5:6

*For in Jesus Christ neither circumcision availeth any thing, nor uncircumcision; but faith which worketh by love.* (Underline mine)

## Colossians 1:8

*Who also declared unto us your love in the Spirit.* (Underline mine)

From the above underlined scriptures you can see that, "*...Faith worketh by love...,*" "*Love never fails...*" and we are to "*...love in the Spirit...*" It follows that we have to continually yield to the Holy Spirit to impart us.

*John 4:24*

<u>God is a Spirit</u>: *and they that worship him must worship him <u>in spirit</u> and in truth.* (Underline mine)

We are created in the image and likeness of God. Therefore, we need to be fully connected to the Holy Spirit in all we do because God is a Spirit or Holy Spirit.

## 13. Love of the Spirit

*Romans 15:30*

*Now I beseech you, brethren, for the Lord Jesus Christ's sake, and for the <u>love of the Spirit</u>, that ye strive together with me in your prayers to God for me;* (Underline mine)

God is love, Jesus is love, and the Holy Spirit is also love. The Trinity is love. Pursuing intimacy with the Holy Spirit and the love of God will be enormously shed abroad in your heart by the Holy Ghost. We are to also love.

## 14. The Spirit of Judgment

*Isaiah 4:4*

*When the <u>Lord</u> shall have washed away the filth of the daughters of Zion, and shall have purged the blood of Jerusalem from the midst thereof by the <u>spirit of judgment</u>, and by the <u>spirit of burning</u>.* (Underline mine)

Can you spot the difference between this scripture and Isaiah 4:2 I made reference to earlier on to illustrate the use of *LORD, Lord, and lord* in the Bible depending on verse and translation? Both scriptures are within a close range, in the same passage in Isaiah, in the Old Testament which suggests that Isaiah 4:2 "LORD" shouldn't have been different from Isaiah 4:4 "Lord" which I underlined above, but it is different. Can you see they are used *interchangeably*? Shouldn't both of them have been "LORD" since they are both within the same passage, the same Isaiah, the same Old Testament, and the same translation? There seems to be inconsistency. In my curiosity, I checked many translations including AMPC, NKJV, NAS, and NIV and found out their Isaiah 4:4 were also put down as "Lord."

Now let's move on. Can you also see that I underlined *"spirit of judgment"* and *"spirit of burning"* above? Even though they both came with "spirit" with small letter 's', they are of God. Not human spirit or evil spirit. AMPC, NKJV, NAS, and NIV all also put it down as "spirit."

## John 16:8

*And when he is come, he will reprove the world of sin, and of righteousness, and of judgment:*

The Holy Spirit knows how to pierce through stony hearts of hardened criminals, the wicked, atheists to convict them of sin and judge them to receive salvation. I have already stated in number 21 point of Chapter one that the Holy Spirit is a very effective agent for evangelism.

## 15. The Spirit of burning

From Isaiah 4:4, we see that the Holy Spirit is a burning Spirit. How? The Holy Spirit will act as a pruning, purging, and refining agent in a believer's life. The Bible says in:

## Malachi 3:2-3

*² But who may abide the day of his coming?*
*and who shall stand when he appeareth?*
*for he is like a <u>refiner's fire, and like fullers' soap</u>:*

*³ And he shall sit as a <u>refiner and purifier</u> of silver:*
*and he shall <u>purify</u> the sons of Levi, and <u>purge</u> them as gold and silver, that they may offer unto the LORD an offering in righteousness.* (Underline mine)

The Holy Spirit works in the life of a believer who will co-operate and yield to get rid of every chaff, bad habits and character, hindering progress. The Bible says "...*Christ liveth in me...*" He says again, "...*Christ in me, the hope of glory.*" Christ will not dwell in a filthy place because He says again, "*Your body is the temple of the Holy Spirit.*" There has to be a total cleansing because, "...*He that is in you is greater than he that is in the world.*"

## Matthew 3:11

*I indeed baptize you with water unto repentance: but he that cometh after me is mightier than I, whose shoes I am not worthy to bear: he shall baptize you with the* <u>Holy Ghost, and with fire:</u> (Underline mine)

The above scripture says that Jesus baptised with the Holy Ghost and with fire. The fire will burn everything not of God. Shadrach, Meshach, and Abednego went through the burning fiery furnace fire in Daniel Chapter 3, but came out unhurt and better people. The refining fire is to make us better people.

## 16. The Spirit of glory

### 1 Peter 4:12-14

¹² *Beloved, think it not strange concerning the fiery trial which is to try you, as though some strange thing happened unto you:*

¹³ *But rejoice, inasmuch as ye are partakers of Christ's sufferings; that, when his glory shall be revealed, ye may be glad also with exceeding joy.*

¹⁴ <u>*If ye be reproached for the name of Christ*</u>, *happy are ye; for* <u>*the spirit of glory*</u> *and of God resteth upon you: on their part he is evil spoken of, but on your part he is glorified.* (Underline mine)

The above scripture reassures us that if we are reproached and persecuted for the name of Christ, we should be happy because we will eventually be victorious in Christ Jesus and the Spirit of glory will rest upon us. Hallelujah! The attacks, trials, persecutions will be turned into a testimony. As long as you are promoting the kingdom of God, and preaching the gospel of Christ, there will be resistance from the enemy. God will overthrow the works of the devil. Don't try to defend yourself. Hand everything to God, and the glory of God will manifest in your life.

## 1 Peter 2:23

*Who, when he was reviled, reviled not again; when he suffered, he threatened not; but committed himself to him that judgeth righteously:*

Don't answer back your accusers, persecutors, critics, adversaries, and enemies. The battle is the Lord's. God will fight for you, and you will hold your peace. The Spirit of glory will be imparted on you by the Holy Spirit as you hold your peace.

## 17. The seven Spirits

### Revelation 1:4

*John to the seven churches which are in Asia: Grace be unto you, and peace, from him which is, and which was, and which is to come; and from <u>the seven Spirits</u> which are before his throne;* (Underline mine)

### Revelation 3:1

*And unto the angel of the church in Sardis write; These things saith he that hath the <u>seven Spirits of God</u>, and the seven stars; I know thy works, that thou hast a name that thou livest, and art dead.* (Underline mine)

The above two scriptures confirm that there are seven Spirits of God. One Holy Spirit manifesting in seven ways, plus much more as we have seen from our discussion above. The Holy Spirit of God is one but He manifests in us and through us in many different ways including positive and negative dimensions.

## CONCLUSION

*1 John 4:1-2*

*¹Beloved, believe not every spirit, <u>but try the spirits whether they are of God</u>: because many false prophets are gone out into the world.*

*² Hereby know ye the Spirit of God: Every spirit that confesseth that Jesus Christ is come in the flesh is of God:* (Underline mine)

Now we know that we have different types of Spirit and spirit, and different ways of manifestation, from our discussion above. We must be prepared to discern, know, and be conscious of the kind of Spirit or spirit in operation at any given point in time. How? Test all Spirit or spirit. With what? The Word of God as prescribed in the above scripture. It says "*…but try the spirits whether they are of God…*" From our earlier discussions, you know now that both positive and negative, Holy Spirit, evil spirit, and lying spirit also proceed from God, as well as other sources as we will find out in more detail in subsequent chapters soon. Try all Spirit and spirit!

Avoid falling into error because you don't know what the scriptures says. Be a competent Bible Scholar. Read what Jesus said to the Sadducees in:

*Matthew 22:29*

*Jesus answered and said unto them, Ye do err, not knowing the scriptures, nor the power of God.*

Oh! What a terrible state to be in. To err is to be in error or make mistakes. Sadly speaking, is this not the position of some believers?

Busy with everything in the world minus Bible study. How can somebody commune well with the Holy Spirit and triumph over evil spirits when they are devoid of the sword of the Spirit? Jesus said in:

## Luke 10:42

*<u>But one thing is needful</u>: and Mary hath chosen that good part, which shall not be taken away from her.* (Underline mine)

How many things are needed in life? One thing! And that's Bible study. Avoid making unnecessary avoidable mistakes in life by equipping yourself in advance with the truth in the Word of God which no demon spirit can mess up. The Bible says again in: *Galatians 5:25, "If we live in the Spirit, let us also walk in the Spirit."*

# CHAPTER FOUR

# THE HUMAN SPIRIT, SOUL, AND BODY

*1 Thessalonians 5:23*

*And the very God of peace sanctify you wholly; and I pray God your whole <u>spirit and soul and body</u> be preserved blameless unto the coming of our Lord Jesus Christ.* (Underline mine)

The above is my sincere prayer for everyone that reads this book in Jesus' name. Amen! Apostle Paul, confirms with this scripture that man is made up of three parts. That is, spirit, soul, and body. Some refer to man as being *tripartite* in nature. Meaning that man is a spirit, has a soul, and lives in a body. These three parts of man are so united and fused together that you cannot separate them.

This book is basically about the Holy Spirit, but because the Holy Spirit interacts with man, and especially the spirit of man, it has become absolutely important for me to also discuss the three components of man as we discuss the Holy Spirit. This will further help expose the relationship between the Holy Spirit and man.

## THE HUMAN SPIRIT

Is the Holy Spirit the same as the human spirit? Absolutely not the same. The Holy Spirit is God, and therefore, superior to human spirit. We have already seen in earlier chapters some of the characteristics of the Holy Spirit. Those features already suggest to us that both spirits are different.

However, note that the Holy Spirit and human spirit are *similar* in the sense that they are both invisible, intangible, and eternal or everlasting in nature. Spirits don't die, but they can relocate. You will get to see that when we deal with unclean spirits.

As discussed in Chapter one, another major way of differentiating them scripturally is to note that the Holy Spirit is a person, and therefore, should always be referred to with the pronoun 'He' or 'Him', but not 'It', and must always be written with a capital letter 'S.' For example, Holy Spirit or Holy Ghost. On the other hand, the human spirit should always be written with a small letter 's.' Evil spirits should also be written with small letter 's' in the Bible.

It is important to always pay attention to whether your Bible used 'Spirit' or 'spirit' in a verse, or passage in order to be sure the kind of spirit that is being referred to. I have observed that sometimes different translations use them interchangeably, and it ought not to be so especially when you really want to be sure the kind of spirit the Bible is referring to.

*Where does the human spirit go to after death?* The Bible says in:

## Ecclesiastes 12:7

*Then shall the dust return to the earth as it was: <u>and the spirit shall return unto God who gave it.</u>* (Underline mine)

The above scripture tells us that when man dies, the human spirit returns back to our Creator who gave the spirit. The spirit of man goes to be with the Lord. You can see the spirit of man *relocating* here. May his spirit rest in peace. Amen!

For a better understanding of what the human spirit truly looks like, I will like to further break it down into three types as follows:

## THE NATURAL MAN, CARNAL MAN, AND MATURE CHRISTIAN HUMAN SPIRIT

## The natural man human spirit

Who is this natural man? Let me describe him for you. This man's spirit is still spiritually dead. He does not believe there is God. He says he is an atheist. He has not given his life to Jesus because he does not believe. The Holy Spirit can only interact with this natural man to convict him to surrender his life to Jesus. This is how the Bible described him in:

*Psalms 14:1*

<u>*The fool hath said in his heart, There is no God*</u>*. They are corrupt, they have done abominable works, there is none that doeth good.* (Underline mine)

This natural man's spirit is not regenerated because he has not accepted Jesus as his Lord and Savior. He is not born again. This man is in the flesh, operating from his five senses of smell, hearing, taste, sight, and touch.

*1 John 2:15-17*

[15] *Love not the world, neither the things that are in the world. If any man love the world, the love of the Father is not in him.*

[16] *For all that is in the world, the lust of the flesh, and the lust of the eyes, and the pride of life, is not of the Father, but is of the world.*

[17] *And the world passeth away, and the lust thereof: but he that doeth the will of God abideth for ever.*

The natural man loves the world. He does not believe in God or miracles. He believes in Science and Technology. His slogan is "Seeing is believing." Not believing in to see.

## 1 Corinthians 2:14

*14 <u>But the natural man</u> receiveth not the things of the Spirit of God: for they are foolishness unto him: neither can he know them, because they are spiritually discerned.* (Underline mine)

## The carnal or sensual man human spirit

Who is this carnal or sensual man? This man is born again with regenerated human spirit, and indwelling of the Holy Spirit. He has not yet been filled with the Holy Spirit or baptism of the Holy Spirit. Therefore, he does not speak in tongues. He rarely engages in spiritual exercises like Bible study, meditation, fasting, prayers, praise, worship, church fellowship, and does not honor God with his tithe. As a result, this Christian is not growing and the Holy Spirit is unable to interact with his human spirit properly, because the Holy Spirit has been grieved, ignored, and made dormant. This person is a lukewarm Christian.

## Revelation 3:16

*So then because <u>thou art lukewarm,</u> and neither cold nor hot, I will spue thee out of my mouth.* (Underline mine)

## Hebrews 5:12-14

*12 For when for the time ye ought to be teachers, ye have need that one teach you again which be the first principles of the oracles of God; and are become such as have need of milk, and not of strong meat.*

*13 For every one that useth milk is unskilful in the word of righteousness: for he is a babe.*

*14 But strong meat belongeth to them that are of full age, even those who by reason of use have their senses exercised to discern both good and evil.*

The above scripture is simply encouraging new born babes in Christ to keep studying the Bible to grow and become teachers. Grow from the stage of drinking the milk of the Word of God as you are taught, to mature eating strong meat as you become a competent teacher. There must not be a backsliding, or stagnation in the spiritual life of a born again Christian. The Bible says we are to shine brighter and brighter, from glory to glory. Hallelujah!

## Proverbs 4:18

*But the path of the just is as the shining light, that shineth more and more unto the perfect day.*

Read below how Apostle Paul admonished carnal born again Christians in the *Corinthian church*.

## 1 Corinthians 3:1-3

*[1] And I, brethren, could not speak unto you as unto spiritual, but as unto <u>carnal</u>, even as unto <u>babes in Christ</u>.*

*[2] <u>I have fed you with milk, and not with meat:</u> for hitherto ye were not able to bear it, neither yet now are ye able.*

*[3] <u>For ye are yet carnal</u>: for whereas there is among you envying, and strife, and divisions, are ye not <u>carnal</u>, and walk as men?* (Underline mine)

Apostle Paul went further and gave a catalogue of things these carnal Christians in the Corinthian church needs to be aware of. He also spelt out the consequence of indulging in such practices. He says such people will not inherit the kingdom of God

## 1 Corinthians 6:9-10

*[9] <u>Know ye not that the unrighteous shall not inherit the kingdom of God</u>? Be not deceived: neither fornicators, nor*

*idolaters, nor adulterers, nor effeminate, nor abusers of themselves with mankind,*

¹⁰ *Nor thieves, nor covetous, nor drunkards, nor revilers, nor extortioners, shall inherit the kingdom of God.* (Underline mine)

Read below how Apostle Paul admonished the carnal Christians in the *Galatian church*. They were born again Spirit filled Christians, but later began to backslide so much that they started manifesting fleshly worldly lifestyle, and Apostle Paul cried out saying in:

## Galatians 3:1-3

¹ <u>*O foolish Galatians,*</u> *who hath bewitched you, that ye should not obey the truth, before whose eyes Jesus Christ hath been evidently set forth, crucified among you?*

² *This only would I learn of you, Received ye the Spirit by the works of the law, or by the hearing of faith?*

³ <u>*Are ye so foolish? having begun in the Spirit, are ye now made perfect by the flesh*</u>*?* (Underline mine)

Apostle Paul went further and gave a catalogue of things these carnal Christians in the Galatian church needs to be aware of. He also spelt out the consequence of indulging in such practices. He says the people who practice such things will not inherit the kingdom of God.

## Galatians 5:19-21

¹⁹ *Now the works of the flesh are manifest, which are these; Adultery, fornication, uncleanness, lasciviousness,*

²⁰ *Idolatry, witchcraft, hatred, variance, emulations, wrath, strife, seditions, heresies,*

²¹ *Envyings, murders, drunkenness, revellings, and such like: of the which I tell you before, as I have also told you in time past, that <u>they which do such things shall not inherit the kingdom of God</u>.* (Underline mine)

The scripture below makes it clear that to be carnally minded is death. Now you can see it is a very dangerous ground to tread on to be a carnal Christian.

*Romans 8:6*

<u>*For to be carnally minded is death*</u>; *but to be spiritually minded is life and peace.* (Underline mine)

### The mature Christian human spirit

This mature Christian or spiritual man intentionally and deliberately engages in spiritual exercises like Bible study, meditation, fasting, prayers, praise, worship, and church fellowship. He speaks in tongues, and also honors God with his tithe. He also tries his best to avoid sin, and improve his character towards God and men. He loves God, and promotes the kingdom of God. He is a good ambassador of Christ. The Holy Spirit finds it easier to interact with this person's human spirit.

### THE HUMAN UNCLEAN AND CLEAN SPIRIT

It sounds weird that a human being can have either *unclean* or *clean* spirit. Doesn't it? I think it does, and to be with an unclean spirit is not a comfortable situation to be in as we will find out now. Let us now proceed further to investigate and clarify this.

### Human unclean spirit

*Mark 5:1-13*

¹ *And they came over unto the other side of the sea, into the country of the Gadarenes.*

*² And when he was come out of the ship, immediately there met him out of the tombs <u>a man with an unclean spirit</u>,*

*³ Who had his dwelling among the tombs; and no man could bind him, no, not with chains:*

*⁴ Because that he had been often bound with fetters and chains, and the chains had been plucked asunder by him, and the fetters broken in pieces: neither could any man tame him.*

*⁵ And always, night and day, he was in the mountains, and in the tombs, crying, and cutting himself with stones.*

*⁶ But when he saw Jesus afar off, he ran and worshipped him,*

*⁷ <u>And cried with a loud voice, and said</u>, What have I to do with thee, Jesus, thou Son of the most high God? I adjure thee by God, that thou torment me not.*

*⁸ <u>For he said unto him, Come out of the man, thou unclean spirit.</u>*

*⁹ <u>And he asked him, What is thy name? And he answered, saying, My name is Legion: for we are many.</u>*

*¹⁰ <u>And he besought him much that he would not send them away out of the country.</u>*

*¹¹ Now there was there nigh unto the mountains a great herd of swine feeding.*

*¹² And all the devils besought him, saying, Send us into the swine, that we may enter into them.*

*¹³ And forthwith Jesus gave them leave. <u>And the unclean spirits went out, and entered into the swine</u>: and the herd ran violently down a steep place into the sea, (they were about two thousand;) <u>and were choked in the sea</u>.* (Underline mine)

The above is the story of a mad man in the country of the Gadarenes. Please note the following:

*First*, I would like you to note that verse 2 says that this mad man had an *"unclean spirit."* And that's why the spirit is written with small letter 's' because it is not Holy Spirit. It is human unclean spirit.

*Second*, verse 7 tells us that unclean spirits speak. *"And cried with a loud voice, and said…"* Now you know unclean spirit speaks, and you need the *gift of discerning of spirits* to pick that up. We will deal with this in a subsequent chapter.

*Third*, in verse 8, Jesus discerned that the man had an unclean spirit and commanded him *"For he said unto him, Come out of the man, thou unclean spirit."*

*Fourth*, in Verse 9, Jesus went further, *"And he asked him, What is thy name? And he answered, saying, My name is Legion: for we are many."* The unclean spirit in the man said his name is Legion and they are many. A legion is about 3 to 6 thousand.

*Fifth*, in Verse 10, the unclean spirit begged Jesus thus, *"And he besought him much that he would not send them away out of the country."* I told you earlier that unclean spirits, devil, or demon spirits can *relocate*. Here this unclean spirit besought Jesus not to cast him out to a foreign country, but into swine. We saw in the Preface and Chapter one of this book that the Holy Spirit from the LORD departed from King Saul. To where? This shows that both the unclean spirit and the Holy Spirit from the LORD can relocate.

## 1 Samuel 16:14

<u>But the Spirit of the LORD departed from Saul</u>, *and an evil spirit from the LORD troubled him.* (Underline mine)

I would like to also mention this about the relocation of the Holy Spirit while we are discussing this here. Jesus said this about the Comforter or Holy Spirit in:

## John 16:7

*Nevertheless I tell you the truth; It is expedient for you that I go away: for if I go not away, <u>the Comforter will not come unto you</u>; but if I depart, <u>I will send him unto you</u>.* (Underline mine)

The statement Jesus made in the above scripture clearly shows that the Holy Spirit does relocate. Jesus said, "*... the comforter will not come unto you*". From where? He says again, "*... I will send him unto you.*" Again, from where? *Is this not a relocation* of the Holy Spirit?

**Sixth,** verse 13 says, *And forthwith Jesus gave them leave. And the unclean spirits went out, and entered into the swine: and the herd ran violently down a steep place into the sea, (they were about two thousand;) and were choked in the sea.*

Jesus cast out the unclean spirits and they relocated into swine, and they were choked in the sea. Can you see Jesus' Spirit communicating with the unclean spirit here? This shows that spirits interact with spirits. Did it not baffle you that Jesus was communicating with an unclean invisible, intangible spirit?

When the coronavirus, COVID 19 started, one hypothesis suggests that this deadly virus which led to a worldwide pandemic originated from Wuhan seafood market in China. Can you see that viruses, bacteria, germs are deadly? They left the mad man into the swine and about two thousand of them died. What do you think will happen to a person who eats the swine with the unclean spirit? The unclean spirit can be transferred to that person because spirits don't die.

*Matthew 12:43-45*

⁴³ *<u>When the unclean spirit is gone out of a man</u>, he walketh through dry places, seeking rest, and findeth none.*

⁴⁴ *Then he saith, I will return into my house from whence I came out; and when he is come, he findeth it empty, swept, and garnished.*

⁴⁵ *Then goeth he, <u>and taketh with himself seven other spirits more wicked than himself</u>, and they enter in and dwell there: and the last state of that man is worse than the first. Even so shall it be also unto this wicked generation.* (Underline mine)

We see again in the above scripture that a man can have unclean spirit. What's the *solution* to deal with this sort of situation?

*Mark 16:17-18*

¹⁷ *And these signs shall follow them that believe; <u>In my name shall they cast out devils</u>; they shall speak with new tongues;*

¹⁸ *They shall take up serpents; and if they drink any deadly thing, it shall not hurt them; they shall lay hands on the sick, and they shall recover.* (Underline mine)

*Luke 10:19*

*Behold, I give unto you power to tread on serpents and scorpions, and over all the power of the enemy: and nothing shall by any means hurt you.*

**First**, unclean spirits should be cast out by faith in the name of Jesus. That's what Jesus commanded us to do in Mark 16:17 above. And in Luke 10:19, He gave us power to tread on the enemy fearlessly. However, I have to also mention here that to be able to do this effectively requires being born again, filled with the Holy Spirit, and the power of God, and also having an intimate relationship with the Holy Spirit. If not, what happened to the 7 sons of Sceva may repeat itself. Evil spirit spoke saying in:

## Acts 19:15

*And the evil spirit answered and said, Jesus I know, and Paul I know; but who are ye?*

**Second**, Jesus said in Mark 16:18 above that if we drink any deadly thing it will not hurt us. In addition to that, it is vital to always bless your food and drinks before you eat. A simple prayer like this will do. *"I bless this food and drink. As I eat by faith, I declare this meal will nourish my body in Jesus' name. Amen!"*

## Proverbs 4:23

*Keep thy heart with all diligence; for out of it are the issues of life.*

**Third**, you have to deliberately ensure you protect your heart from being polluted, making sure you only see, hear, say, smell, and touch things that will edify you. Avoid junks and all ungodly sinful things. Be careful what you see and hear on TV, internet, social media etc. Read what King David said in:

## Psalms 101:2-3

[2] *I will behave myself wisely in a perfect way. O when wilt thou come unto me?*
*I will walk within my house with a perfect heart.*

[3] *I will set no wicked thing before mine eyes:* *I hate the work of them that turn aside; it shall not cleave to me.* (Underline mine)

King David says in verse 2 above, *"I will behave myself wisely in a perfect way."* This means he will behave himself in a godly way through self-discipline and the power of the Holy Spirit. He says again, *"I will walk within my house with a perfect heart."* This means that his thoughts, words, and actions at home are godly. He is not two faced. His behaviour indoors and outdoors are the same. In verse 3, he says, *"I will set no wicked thing before mine eyes:"* This means that he will not set before his eyes violent, corrupt, immoral, and pornographic TV, social media, and internet programmes. Why? Because they will depress, corrupt, and quench his human spirit. King David will rather set before his eyes his Bible, meditate, fast, pray, praise, and worship God. This will revive his human spirit. Always protect your spirit, and sharpen yourself spiritually because the Bible says in:

## Proverbs 18:14

*The spirit of a man will sustain his infirmity; but a wounded spirit who can bear?*

## Human clean spirit

A born again Christian with recreated spirit, having received the life of Jesus Christ, and has both indwelling and infilling of the Holy Spirit, with evidence of speaking in tongues, has human clean spirit. We saw in the Preface section of this book that Apostle Peter and Paul were filled with the Holy Spirit, and Jesus was filled with the Holy Spirit without measure.

Being filled with the Holy Spirit with evidence of speaking in tongues helps a born again Christian to discern or perceive spirits and things. In Acts 5:1-11, Apostle Peter accurately discerned that Ananias and Sapphira kept back part of the price of their sold possessions. In Acts 14:6-10, Apostle Paul perceived that a cripple man had faith to walk, and ministered to him, and he was healed and walked. In Mark 2:8, Jesus perceived in His spirit the thoughts of the scribes. These people were able to operate with such accurate precision because they had a human clean spirit filled with the Holy Spirit.

We have already seen in Chapter one that in the Old Testament in Genesis 41:38 that Joseph was filled with the Holy Spirit, and in Exodus 31:3, Bazeleel was also filled with the Holy Spirit. The Holy Spirit cannot dwell in a filthy vessel. The fact that these two men were filled with the Holy Spirit is an indication they had a human clean spirit. Let's consider a few more examples.

## Moses

### Numbers 11:25

*<sup>25</sup> And the LORD came down in a cloud, and spake unto him, and took of the <u>spirit</u> that was upon him, and gave it unto the <u>seventy elders</u>: and it came to pass, that, when the <u>spirit</u> rested upon them, they prophesied, and did not cease.* (Underline mine)

### Numbers 11:25 Good News Translation (GNT)

*Then the LORD came down in the cloud and spoke to him. He took some of the <u>spirit</u> he had given to Moses and gave it to the <u>seventy leaders</u>. When the <u>spirit</u> came on them, they began to shout like prophets, but not for long.* (Underline mine)

Numbers 11:25 New International Version (NIV) *Then the LORD came down in the cloud and spoke with him, and he took some of the power of the <u>Spirit</u> that was on him and put it on the <u>seventy elders</u>. When the <u>Spirit</u> rested on them, they prophesied—but did not do so again.* (Underline mine)

I have laid above Numbers 11:25 of KJV, GNT, and NIV and underlined the word spirit. Can you spot the difference? The KJV and GNT put down "spirit" with small letter 's' indicating that it was Moses' human spirit that was transferred to the 70 elders of Israel. This appears to be right. RSV, ISV also got it down as "spirit". However NIV above put it down as "Spirit" with capital letter 'S' indicating that it was Moses' Holy Spirit that was transferred to the 70 elders. This does not appear to be right.

Most modern translations including AMPC, NKJV, NAS, NLT etc. all put it down as "Spirit." Prior to this time in Numbers, did the Bible record anywhere that Moses was filled with the Holy Spirit? Was Moses born again and filled with the Holy Spirit? How could God have taken Moses' Spirit and not his spirit?

Moses had a human clean spirit. That's why God transferred part of it to 70 selected elders to support him in administration of the affairs of the Israelites.

## Elijah

*2 Kings 2:9*

*And it came to pass, when they were gone over, that Elijah said unto Elisha, Ask what I shall do for thee, before I be taken away from thee. And Elisha said, I pray thee, let a double portion of thy <u>spirit</u> be upon me.* (Underline mine)

Elisha asked for Elijah's human spirit in the above scripture. That's why the "spirit" was written with a small letter 's'. Most translations including AMPC, NKJV, NAS, NIV etc all put it down as "spirit."

This Elijah example is a confirmation that the Moses example was also Moses' human spirit. Note that when somebody has a clean human spirit it can be transferred to somebody else. Moses' human clean spirit was transferred to 70 elders. Elijah's human clean spirit was transferred to Elisha. We also discussed before that Moses laid hands on Joshua and transferred the spirit of wisdom to him in Deuteronomy 34:9. On the other hand, Jesus cast out the unclean spirit in the mad man of the country of the Gadarenes. His own spirit was unclean and of no use. Therefore, Jesus cast out the unclean spirit from the mad man into swine.

## Can the human spirit be revived?

Yes, the human spirit can be revived.

## Jacob

*Genesis 45:27*

*And they told him all the <u>words</u> of Joseph, which he had said unto them: and when he saw the <u>wagons</u> which Joseph had sent to carry him, <u>the spirit of Jacob their father revived:</u>* (Underline mine)

Jacob had thought Joseph was dead, and had been sad, but when his children went to Egypt to buy food, they discovered Joseph was still alive. They gave him the good news that they saw Joseph alive, and he saw the wagons Joseph sent to carry him, his spirit revived. Wagon is a vehicle or car like Rolls Royce, Mercedes Benz, Lexus, Jeep, Jaguar etc. I pray that my God will bless you with good news, and wagon cars that will revive your spirit in Jesus' name. Amen!

## There was no more spirit in her

*1 Kings 10:4-5*

*⁴ And when the <u>queen of Sheba</u> had seen all Solomon's wisdom, and the house that he had built,*

*⁵ And the meat of his table, and the sitting of his servants, and the attendance of his ministers, and their apparel, and his cupbearers, and his ascent by which he went up unto the house of the LORD; <u>there was no more spirit in her.</u>* (Underline mine)

The Queen of Sheba heard so much about King Solomon's wisdom, excellence, and wealth. She came with her entourage to meet King Solomon. After she saw King Solomon's splendor and glory, the above scripture says in verse 5 that, *"...there was no more spirit in her."* This appears to be a figure of speech implying that she was overwhelmed, dumbfounded, and astonished.

Note that the Queen of Sheba did not faint or die as the statement, *"...there was no more spirit in her"* suggests in some sense.

Apostle Paul has told us that man is made up of spirit, soul, and body, fused together. The absence of any of the components will result in death. And not even her Majesty Queen of Sheba, or any human being has control over the spirit to stop death. Read what King Solomon said to that effect in:

*Ecclesiastes 8:8*

*<u>There is no man that hath power over the spirit to retain the spirit; neither hath he power in the day of death</u>: and there is no discharge in that war; neither shall wickedness deliver those that are given to it.* (Underline mine)

## Do animals have spirit?

*Ecclesiastes 3:21 New International Version (NIV)*

*Who knows if the human spirit rises upward and if <u>the spirit of the animal</u> goes down into the earth?"* (Underline mine)

The above scripture from (NIV) tells us that animals have spirit. We also saw earlier in Mark Chapter 5, that Jesus cast out unclean spirits from a mad man and sent them into swine. These two biblical references suggest that animals have spirit.

## Interaction between the Holy Spirit and the human spirit

### Old Testament

*Exodus 25:9*

*According to all that I shew thee, after the pattern of the tabernacle, and the pattern of all the instruments thereof, even so shall ye make it.*

In the Old Testament, God dwelt in temples and tabernacles. These were built according to the pattern prescribed by God. Usually the Temples had three parts – The outer court, holy place, and holy of holies. Everyone had access to the outer court. The priests had access to the holy place. Only the high priest had access to the holy of holies chamber. This is where they kept the mercy seat, and the ark of the covenant of the Lord. This place is highly consecrated to the Lord.

Every year, the high priest goes into the holy of holies with the blood of goats, and bulls to sacrifice and make *atonement* for his own sins and the sins of the people.

### *Exodus 29:45-46*

[45] *And I will dwell <u>among</u> the children of Israel, and will be their God.*

[46] *And they shall know that I am the LORD their God, that brought them forth out of the land of Egypt, that I may dwell <u>among</u> them: I am the LORD their God.* (Underline mine)

The above scripture further tells us that God dwelt *among* the people.

## New Testament

### *2 Corinthians 6:16*

*And what agreement hath the temple of God with idols? for ye are the temple of the living God; as God hath said, I will dwell <u>in</u> them, and walk <u>in</u> them; and I will be their God, and they shall be my people.* (Underline mine)

In the New Testament, God dwells *in* the saints of God, and the scripture above confirms that. Once a person is born again, with regenerated spirit, there will be indwelling of the Holy Spirit *in* the person.

The Bible says, "*...Christ liveth in me...*", "*...Christ in me the hope of glory*", "*Your body is the temple of the Holy Spirit which* *is **in** you...*", "*Greater is he that is in you than he that is in the world*" "*God worketh **in** you both to will and to do of his good pleasure*", "*...The kingdom of God is **within** you,*" *and* "*...He which hath begun a good work **in** you will perform it until the day of Jesus Christ.*"

As a believer, born again saint of God, the Holy Spirit now dwells *within* you. This enables interaction between the Holy Spirit and the human spirit.

## Proverbs 20:27

*The spirit of man is the candle of the LORD, searching all the inward parts of the belly.*

A person who is not born again is dead spiritually. The Holy Spirit can only convict him to give his life to Jesus. And then, there can be further interaction between the two spirits. An unbeliever, or atheist is not likely to operate beyond the flesh, sense realm because they are not born again. No indwelling of the Holy Spirit.

On the other hand, the human spirit of born again Christians serves as a candle, light, illumination of the LORD, to search all our inward parts. This is made possible because the born again Christian spirit is regenerated, and Christ has been received, and the Holy Spirit dwells in this person, and interacts with the human spirit.

## Romans 8:16

*The Spirit itself beareth witness with our spirit, that we are the children of God:* (Underline mine).

You can see from the above scripture that the first "Spirit" is written with capital letter 'S' which means the Holy Spirit. The second "spirit" is written with a small letter 's' which indicates human spirit. Bearing of witness denotes interaction.

This scripture makes it clear that the Holy Spirit Himself interacts with our human spirit. He bears witness with our spirit that we are born again children of God to be favored and blessed.

## Similarities between the Holy Spirit and the human spirit

- They are both spirits
- They are both invisible
- They are both intangible
- They are both eternal and everlasting in nature
- The Holy Spirit interacts with the human spirit of a believer
- They both have the characteristics of a person. That is, they both have mind, emotions, and will (MEW). Man's MEW is in the soul.
- Both of them can relocate

## Differences between the Holy Spirit and the human spirit

- The Holy Spirit, Holy Ghost, or Spirit should always be written with capital letter 'S', while the human spirit should always be written with small letter 's'. Note that *Spirit* and *spirit* are sometimes used *interchangeably*, but they are not exactly the same as you have seen so far in this book.
- The Holy Spirit is *God*, and a member of the Trinity, but a human being is just a *god* – Psalm 82:6. Note the difference – Capital letter 'G' and small letter 'g'.
- Every human being is born with a spirit, but you must be born again, accept Jesus Christ as your Lord and Savior, with a regenerated spirit to have indwelling of the Holy Spirit.

# THE HUMAN SOUL

*3 John 1:2*

*Beloved, I wish above all things that thou mayest prosper and be in health, even as thy soul prospereth.*

My prayer for you is that you will continually be in excellent health with a prosperous soul in Jesus' name. Amen! This scripture clearly states that the manifestation of prosperity in a man's life is dependent, and commensurate to his prosperous soul. Therefore, it follows that we have to pay a very good attention to the prosperity of our soul. Embrace the Agape love of Christ and have a prosperous soul.

Just like the human spirit, the human soul is invisible, intangible, and eternal or everlasting in nature. The Greek word for soul is *psyche*, and it means mind. That's the root word for psychology. The soul is made up of the mind, emotions, and will (MEW).

The mind is the center of a man's knowledge and intelligence. The emotions have to do with negative emotions like anger, sorrow, and fear, as well as positive emotions such as love, compassion, peace, and joy. The will of man has to do with the center of where choices and decisions are made. However, as a believer, it is better to surrender your will to the Holy Spirit. The Bible says in:

*Philippians 2:13*

*For it is God which worketh in you both to will and to do of his good pleasure.*

Love is the main thing that the soul needs to operate effectively. Therefore, we must ensure we look after our soul by enhancing it with love, compassion, peace, joy, mercy, kindness, wisdom, reverence, gratitude, gratefulness, forgiveness etc. The Holy Spirit imparts us with the love of God as we yield and co-operate with Him.

**Jonathan loved David wholeheartedly with his soul**

*1 Samuel 18:1*

*And it came to pass, when he had made an end of speaking unto Saul, that the soul of Jonathan was knit with the soul of David, and <u>Jonathan loved him as his own soul</u>.* (Underline mine)

The above scripture tells us that Jonathan loved David as his own soul. That's true love. He further demonstrated the love by giving David gifts. Love is a giver.

The Bible says in:

## Mark 8:36

*For what shall it profit a man, if he shall gain the whole world, and lose his own soul?*

This is a very important question Jesus asked about the soul, and which everyone who desires to have a prosperous soul, as well as for their soul not to perish must answer honestly. Your soul is by far more valuable than all the material things you may acquire in this world. Look after it.

When somebody dies, you hear people say the mantra, *"May his soul rest in peace."* Have you ever wondered why people say that? The reason is because after death, the body decays, but the soul lives on to either end up in heaven or hell eternally. If the soul ends up in heaven, it will rest in peace, but if it ends up in hell, it cannot rest in peace. See Luke 16:19-31 for the parable of the Rich man and Lazarus. The Rich man ended up in hell, while Lazarus ended up in heaven in Abraham's bosom. Brethren, heaven and hell is real.

Therefore, we have a basic duty to look after our soul by making a very important decision to become a born again Christian because this will help open the way to heaven for us. Are you a born again Christian? Give your life to Jesus now. No more excuses!

## John 3:3

*Jesus answered and said unto him, Verily, verily, I say unto thee, Except a man be born again, he cannot see the kingdom of God.*

## Can the soul be cast down?

*Psalms 42:5*

<u>Why art thou cast down, O my soul?</u> *and why art thou disquieted in me?*
*hope thou in God: for I shall yet praise him for the help of his countenance.* (Underline mine)

The above scripture tells us the soul can be cast down. The soul of the Psalmist was depressed, and in despair. What did he do to be refreshed? He put his hope in God praising and trusting the Lord. Praise God!

## Can the soul be restored?

*Psalms 23:3*

<u>*He restoreth my soul*</u>: *he leadeth me in the paths of righteousness for his name's sake.* (Underline mine)

King David tells us in the above scripture that the soul can be restored. God restored his soul. Therefore, no matter how battered the soul may be, believe and trust God for a restoration.

## Similarities between the human spirit and the human soul

- They are both invisible
- They are both intangible
- They are both eternal and everlasting in nature
- They can both be corrupted with sin

## Differences between the human spirit and the human soul

- The human *spirit* and *soul* are sometimes used *interchangeably*, but they are not exactly the same as you have seen so far in this book
- You feed and renew your human spirit with the sword of the Spirit, which is the Word of God – Ephesians 6:17. On the other hand, the human soul needs love to prosper.

## PRAYER FOR YOU

*Psalms 121:7-8*

*⁷ The LORD shall preserve thee from all evil: he shall preserve thy soul.*

*⁸ The LORD shall preserve thy going out and thy coming in from this time forth, and even for evermore.* In Jesus' name. Amen!

## THE HUMAN BODY

Man is a spirit, has a soul, and lives in a body. The body is the *visible* and *tangible* component of the *tripartite* human being. This means that you can *see* and *touch* the body. The body is basically made up of the five senses as follows: touch, hearing, sight, smell, and taste. The body is also referred to as the flesh of man. It is weak and therefore dies and decays. Human beings appear to pay a lot more attention to their corruptible body than their spirit and soul, but it ought not to be so. The realm of the senses is the conscious, natural or ordinary realm.

In order for man to operate at his best, he must deliberately and consciously ensure that he activates the supernatural realm by walking in the Spirit rather than in the flesh or sense realm. The supernatural realm is where you can soar like an eagle doing marvellous things. You experience intuitions, hunches, and inspirations in the subconscious or supernatural realm.

## THINGS TO DO TO HELP YOUR BODY

### 1. Don't defile your body

*1 Corinthians 6:19*

*What? know ye not that your body is the temple of the Holy Ghost which is in you, which ye have of God, and ye are not your own?*

*1 Corinthians 3:16-17*

¹⁶ *Know ye not that ye are the temple of God, and that the Spirit of God dwelleth in you?*

¹⁷ <u>*If any man defile the temple of God, him shall God destroy*</u>; *for the temple of God is holy, which temple ye are.* (Underline mine)

The above scriptures states that our body is the temple of the Holy Spirit. Therefore, keep it holy. The consequence for those who defile their body is that God will destroy them. Besides, if you defile your body beyond a certain threshold, your spirit and soul will also be affected, and they may be forced out and the person will die.

## 2. Don't indulge in the works of the flesh

*Galatians 5:19-21*

¹⁹ <u>*Now the works of the flesh are manifest, which are these*</u>; *Adultery, fornication, uncleanness, lasciviousness,*

²⁰ *Idolatry, witchcraft, hatred, variance, emulations, wrath, strife, seditions, heresies,*

²¹ *Envyings, murders, drunkenness, revellings, and such like: of the which I tell you before, as I have also told you in time past, that* <u>*they which do such things shall not inherit the kingdom of God.*</u> (Underline mine)

Note that in spite of the fact that the Bible referred to the above list as the *works of the flesh*, they also corrupt the soul and spirit because the spirit, soul, and body are fused together and therefore cannot be distinctly separated. They are linked together.

Note also that Paul wrote this epistle to Christians in Galatia. This is to show that Christians must not indulge in any of the above listed works of the flesh. *They are not works of the devil as some people are deceived to believe and quick to claim.* Always say "NO" to the works of the flesh. Resist them. Paul made it clear that people who indulge in such works of the flesh will not inherit the kingdom of God which is heaven. Besides, indulging in such practices will grieve and suppress the Holy Spirit, and will not enable Him impart a person properly.

## 1 Corinthians 9:27

<u>*But I keep under my body, and bring it into subjection*</u>*: lest that by any means, when I have preached to others, I myself should be a castaway.* (Underline mine)

*Solution*: The great Apostle Paul says in the above scripture that we have to bring our body into subjection. We must continually challenge ourselves and have *self-discipline* over the above list of works of the flesh through the power of the Holy Spirit because they will seriously also corrupt the spirit and soul if we do nothing.

## Galatians 5:16

*This I say then, Walk in the Spirit, and ye shall not fulfil the lust of the flesh.*

Always discipline, chasten, buffet, and bring your body into subjection in order to effectively deal with fleshy, carnal, bad habits. Paul said in 1 Corinthians 15:31, "…I die daily." Die daily to such things by saying no to them.

## 3. Don't form weapons against yourself

### Isaiah 54:17

*No weapon that is formed against thee shall prosper; and every tongue that shall rise against thee in judgment thou shalt condemn. This is the heritage of the servants of the LORD, and their righteousness is of me, saith the LORD.*

*1 Corinthians 6:18*

*Flee fornication. Every sin that a man doeth is without the body; but he that committeth fornication sinneth against his own body.*

*1 Thessalonians 4:7*

*For God hath not called us unto uncleanness, but unto holiness.*

Note that weapons formed against us will not prosper, but the ones we form against ourselves will prosper. What weapons do you form against your body? For example, don't abuse your body as a Christian by indulging in *debauchery* (excessive use of alcohol, drugs, and sex) because such weapons are likely to prosper. Don't also engage in Lesbian, Gay, Bisexual, and Transgender (LGBT) practices because the Bible is against it. God has not called us unto uncleanness, but unto holiness.

## 4. Avoid gluttony

Gluttony has to do with excessive indulgence on food and drinks. Avoid it because it can lead to obesity, sickness and diseases. Too much sugar will lead to diabetes. Too much alcohol, smoking, and drugs will lead to liver problems. Sexual immorality leads to sexually transmitted diseases. All these corrupt the body, and grieve the Holy Spirit. Esau sold his birth right to Jacob because of food. Hold your urge for food. Fast and read your Bible.

*Matthew 4:4*

*But he answered and said, It is written, Man shall not live by bread alone, but by every word that proceedeth out of the mouth of God.*

## 5. Avoid tattoos

*Leviticus 19:28 (The Living Bible - TLB)*

*You shall not cut yourselves nor put <u>tattoo</u> marks upon yourselves in connection with funeral rites; I am the Lord.* (Underline mine)

God commanded us not to put tattoo marks upon our bodies in the above TLB scripture. We must respect that. Our body is the temple of the Holy Spirit. Don't defile it. The danger of starting to put tattoos on your body is that once some people start, they don't stop and they end up covering their entire body with tattoos.

One of the consequences of having tattoos all over your body as a Christian is that it could hinder you from getting a good job and also possibly hinder you from getting a good person to marry. Like attracts like. You are likely to attract a tattooed person like you. Note also that tattoos are irreversible.

Try and live your life consciously, and intentionally, in all you do. Always apply the principle of safety first to protect your body. If it's not safe, don't do it. Life does not have a duplicate.

## 6. Present your holy body to God

*Romans 12:1*

*I beseech you therefore, brethren, by the mercies of God, that ye present your bodies a living sacrifice, holy, acceptable unto God, which is your reasonable service.*

We are to present our holy body to God as a living sacrifice. Purity and consecration of the body is absolutely important. If you present unholy body to God, it may be unacceptable by God. Don't abuse your body as a Christian. No blemish on your body.

## 7. Spiritual exercise

*1 Timothy 4:8*

*For bodily exercise profiteth little: but godliness is profitable unto all things, having promise of the life that now is, and of that which is to come.*

Take advantage of the little profit you get from bodily exercise and keep fit. You can even go to the gym. Eat balanced diet. Do regular medical check-ups. Also engage meaningfully with spiritual exercise by doing Bible study, meditation, fasting, prayers, praise, and worship, because it is profitable unto all things. Note that constant spiritual exercise will enable you to live in the Spirit and also walk in the Spirit.

It is our duty to deliberately chasten, discipline, and buffet the flesh in order for us to walk in the spirit realm. If we don't discipline our body, it may turn out to be unruly and remain carnal. Tame your body through self-control. If you don't, it will begin to affect the soul and spirit. Walk in the Spirit.

## 8. The spirit sustains a man's infirmity

*Proverbs 18:14*

*The spirit of a man will sustain his infirmity; but a wounded spirit who can bear?*

The spirit of a man does not die, and that is what sustains the body during infirmity. Therefore, look after your spirit. The body can be sick, die, and decay but not the spirit. Look after your spirit by feeding it with the sword of the Spirit, which is the Word of God.

# CHAPTER FIVE

# THE SUPERNATURAL REALM

Basically, we have two realms. The supernatural, invisible, or spirit realm, and the natural, visible, or physical realm. The supernatural realm is very vast, and unlimited. Many types of spirits known and unknown to man operate in this realm. The spirits can be *positive* or *negative* in nature. The Holy Spirit, angelic entities, evil spirits, familiar spirits, witches, wizards, occult powers, demons, devil, Lucifer, Satan etc all operate in this realm. It is important to note that all the entities operating in this realm are *invisible* and *intangible* in nature.

When you start interacting with spirits in the supernatural realm, you will start having *encounters*. You must be careful as a Christian to interact with the Holy Spirit and other good spirits. Always judge what you see, hear, and encounter with the scriptures, because that is the only way you can establish the authenticity of your encounter. The fruit of the spirit you manifest will also show the kind of spirit you fraternise with, whether it is good or evil spirit because the Bible says in: *Matthew 7:20, "Wherefore by their fruits ye shall know them."*

*Ephesians 6:12*

*For we wrestle not against flesh and blood, but against principalities, against powers, against the rulers of the darkness of this world, against spiritual wickedness in high places.*

The above scripture paints a good picture of what happens in the supernatural realm. However, a man who dwells in the secret place of the Most High God, a man in the Spirit will always be victorious over the works of the devil. This man lives in the Spirit and walks in the Spirit, therefore overcomes the wiles of the enemy with precision.

## *James 5:16*

*Confess your faults one to another, and pray one for another, that ye may be healed. <u>The effectual fervent prayer of a righteous man availeth much.</u>* (Underline mine)

Man is a spirit, has a soul, and lives in a body. Man has the advantage of interacting with both realms through fervent, faith filled prayers, especially praying in the Spirit or tongues. You bombard the spirit realm when you pray in unknown tongues or heavenly language. You destroy the works of the devil, and fix, and align godly things as you pray with this mysterious language.

## *Hebrews 11:3*

*Through faith we understand that the worlds were framed by the word of God, <u>so that things which are seen were not made of things which do appear</u>.* (Underline mine)

## *Romans 1:20*

*For the <u>invisible</u> things of him from the creation of the world are clearly seen, <u>being understood by the things that are made,</u> even his eternal power and Godhead; so that they are without excuse:* (Underline mine)

The visible things we see here on earth are all created, made, or downloaded from the invisible supernatural realm. Before they manifested on earth to be visible, they existed in an invisible supernatural realm. As a Christian, you have to invent and develop a more superior technology to bring down to earth the blessings. Prayer!!!

## Ephesians 1:3

*Blessed be the God and Father of our Lord Jesus Christ, who hath blessed us with all spiritual blessings in heavenly places in Christ:*

The above scripture states that God has blessed us with all spiritual blessings in heavenly places in Christ. The blessings are hanging up there in the supernatural invisible realm. We are to bring them down to this visible realm.

## 1 Kings 18:44

*And it came to pass at the <u>seventh time</u>, that he said, Behold, there ariseth a little cloud out of the sea, like a man's hand. And he said, Go up, say unto Ahab, Prepare thy chariot, and get thee down, that the rain stop thee not.* (Underline mine)

Before it rained in the above verse, Elijah prayed seven times bombarding the supernatural realm with prayers, before a little sign of a cloud like a man's hand showed up. He persisted in prayers until the heavens opened up completely and there was abundance of rain. This is an example of a man bringing down from the supernatural invisible realm rain to this visible natural realm. Pray!!!

## James 5:17-18

*17 Elias was a man subject to like passions as we are, and <u>he prayed</u> earnestly that it might not rain: and it rained not on the earth by the space of three years and six months.*

*18 And he <u>prayed again</u>, and the heaven gave rain, and the earth brought forth her fruit.* (Underline mine)

Elijah prayed and locked up heaven and it did not rain for three and half years. When he was satisfied, he prayed again and opened the heavens and there was abundance of rain. Is this not a supernatural exploit performed by a man?

Bring down abundance of your blessings through the mysterious *praying in tongues technology. Pray!!!* The Bible says in: 1 Thessalonians 5:17, *"Pray without ceasing."* It says again in, *"Luke 18:1, "And he spake a parable unto them to this end, that men ought always to pray, and not to faint;* The church needs to also pray for the saints of God. Acts 12:5 says *"Peter therefore was kept in prison: but prayer was made without ceasing of the church unto God for him."*

What about the great Army General, Joshua? This man commanded the sun and the moon to stand still and they obeyed him.

## Joshua 10:12-13

*12 Then spake Joshua to the LORD in the day when the LORD delivered up the Amorites before the children of Israel, and he said in the sight of Israel,*
<u>*Sun, stand thou still upon Gibeon;*</u>
<u>*and thou, Moon, in the valley of Ajalon.*</u>

*13* <u>*And the sun stood still, and the moon stayed,*</u>
*until the people had avenged themselves upon their enemies. Is not this written in the book of Jasher?*
<u>*So the sun stood still in the midst of heaven,*</u>
*and hasted not to go down about a whole day.* (Underline mine)

Elijah and Joshua operated in the Old Testament and performed such supernatural feats. They were natural men, no recreated spirit, and not born again Christians. Therefore, they did not have indwelling of the Holy Spirit, neither did they have infilling of the Holy Spirit. Yet they performed such supernatural feats. As born again Christians, we need to be challenged to grow and step up the game. Jesus made it clear to us in:

## John 14:12

*Verily, verily, I say unto you, He that believeth on me, the works that I do shall he do also; and greater works than these shall he do; because I go unto my Father.*

Let me give you a simple analogy to help you understand what it is like to be in the supernatural realm or in the Spirit. Two nations A and B are on the battlefield. Nation A has well trained Air force pilots and Jet bombers which they use to rain down bombs, and missiles on Nation B. (They are in the Spirit operating from the supernatural realm so to say.) But Nation B only has ground military troops with AK 47 guns and artillery operating in the physical or natural realm. (They are in the flesh so to say.) Who will win this battle? Nation A or B? Of course Nation A. I believe this analogy will challenge you to step up and sharpen your spirit to be in the Spirit operating from the supernatural realm so that you can win all your battles with ease. The Bible says in:

## Isaiah 40:31

*But they that wait upon the LORD shall renew their strength; they shall mount up with wings as eagles; they shall run, and not be weary; and they shall walk, and not faint.*

An eagle is a bird known for mastery in the atmosphere. It soars as high as mountain tops where no other bird will ever dare to near. The eagle is a supernatural bird when compared to other birds, and ground animals. Can you see why ground animals such as fowls, goats, rats, rabbits, and ducks don't have a chance when the eagle strikes? Can you also see that this scenario looks like the Nation A and B analogy picture I painted for you?

Do you want to start operating from the supernatural realm? Wait upon the Lord. Start spiritual exercises of Bible study, meditation, fasting, prayers, praise, and worship. This will help you mount up with wings as eagles to start soaring in the supernatural realm.

# EVIL SPIRITS AND MAGICAL POWERS

In this section, we will go deeper to examine the nature, operations, and procedures (*Modus operandi - Latin*) of evil spirits and magical powers in the spirit realm. These includes familiar spirits, witches, wizards, occult powers, demons, devil, Lucifer, Satan, astrological powers, charms, sorcery, soothsaying, necromancy, enchantment, voodoos, the spirit of divination of gods etc. This Bible says in:

### *Deuteronomy 18:10-13*

[10] *There shall not be found among you any one that maketh his son or his daughter to pass through the fire, or that useth divination, or an observer of times, or an enchanter, or a witch,*

[11] *Or a charmer, or a consulter with familiar spirits, or a wizard, or a necromancer.*

[12] <u>*For all that do these things are an abomination unto the LORD*</u>: *and because of these abominations the LORD thy God doth drive them out from before thee.*

[13] *Thou shalt be perfect with the LORD thy God.* (Underline mine)

The above scripture says that all that engage in the above evil and magical activities are an abomination to the LORD. A Christian must not partake in any of the above listed practices because it's wicked and an abomination unto the LORD. The only reason why I am sharing it with you in this book is for you to be aware that they exist and for you to know how to also deal with them. The Bible says in:

### *2 Corinthians 2:11*

*Lest Satan should get an advantage of us: for we are not ignorant of his devices.*

We must not be ignorant of the devices, and tricks of the devil. As a Christian, you have to be ahead of the devil, and overcome him. Let's look at a few examples from the Bible to demonstrate this.

## Witchcraft - Saul goes to a witch

*1 Samuel 28:3-15*

*³ <u>Now Samuel was dead</u>, and all Israel had lamented him, and buried him in Ramah, even in his own city. And Saul had put away those that had familiar spirits, and the wizards, out of the land.....*

*⁷ <u>Then said Saul unto his servants</u>, Seek me a woman that hath a familiar spirit, that I may go to her, and enquire of her. And his servants said to him, Behold, there is a <u>woman that hath a familiar spirit at Endor</u>.*

*⁸ And Saul disguised himself, and put on other raiment, and he went, and two men with him, and they came to the woman by night: and he said, I pray thee, divine unto me by the familiar spirit, and bring me him up, whom I shall name unto thee....*

*¹¹ <u>Then said the woman, Whom shall I bring up unto thee? And he said, Bring me up Samuel</u>....*

*¹⁵ <u>And Samuel said to Saul, Why hast thou disquieted me, to bring me up? And Saul answered, I am sore distressed;</u> for the Philistines make war against me, and God is departed from me, and answereth me no more, neither by prophets, nor by dreams: therefore I have called thee, that thou mayest make known unto me what I shall do. (Underline mine)*

In our earlier discussion, I said spirits do not die. You can see here that through familiar spirit and witchcraft, a dead person, Samuel's spirit was brought up for interaction. Witchcraft!

Verse 3 tells us Samuel was dead. Verse 7 tells us Saul went to a woman with a familiar spirit or witch. Verse 15, tells us the spirit of Samuel was brought up by the woman, and he spoke with Saul. This was made possible by magical evil powers.

## Magical powers - Aaron's rod swallows pharaoh's men's rods

*Exodus 7:8-12*

*⁸ And the LORD spake unto Moses and unto Aaron, saying,*

*⁹ When <u>Pharaoh</u> shall speak unto you, saying, Shew a miracle for you: then thou shalt say unto Aaron, Take thy rod, and cast it before Pharaoh, and it shall become a serpent.*

*¹⁰ And Moses and Aaron went in unto Pharaoh, and they did so as the LORD had commanded: <u>and Aaron cast down his rod before Pharaoh, and before his servants, and it became a serpent.</u>*

*¹¹ Then Pharaoh also called the wise men and the <u>sorcerers</u>: now the <u>magicians</u> of Egypt, they also did in like manner with their enchantments.*

*¹² <u>For they cast down every man his rod, and they became serpents: but Aaron's rod swallowed up their rods.</u>* (Underline mine)

Can you see power tussle in operation in the above biblical passage between godly men Moses and Aaron, and ungodly men, the sorcerers and magicians? And the godly men won. Note that it may be hard to distinguish between *miracle* of God and *magical* evil powers. That's why we need the *gift of discerning of spirit*. Miracle is superior and it is of God. Magic is inferior and it is of the devil. A test of powers.

## Sorcery - Magical power by Simon

*Acts 8:9-13*

*⁹ <u>But there was a certain man, called Simon</u>, which beforetime in the same city <u>used sorcery, and bewitched the people of Samaria</u>, giving out that himself was some great one:*

*¹⁰ <u>To whom they all gave heed, from the least to the greatest, saying, This man is the great power of God.</u>*

*¹¹ And to him they had regard, because that of long time he had bewitched them with sorceries.*

*¹² But when they believed Philip preaching the things concerning the kingdom of God, and the name of Jesus Christ, they were baptized, both men and women.*

*¹³ Then Simon himself believed also: and when he was baptized, he continued with Philip, and wondered, beholding the miracles and signs which were done.* (Underline mine)

Notice from the above underlined scriptures that Simon the sorcerer bewitched everyone in the city of Samaria. The magical powers Simon displayed in the city of Samaria earned him a lot of respect to the extent that they said in verse 10 above, *"This man is the great power of God."* They could not distinguish between magical powers and the miracle of God.

To prove that the power of God is superior to sorcery, Simon was converted and baptised by Philip. Simon loved evil power and probably bought it with money. That is why he offered Peter money to also get Holy Ghost power, and then Peter told him off because you can't buy the gift of God. See verse 19-20.

## Prince of Persia withstood the angel from delivering Daniel's package

*Daniel 10:12-13*

*¹² <u>Then said he unto me, Fear not, Daniel</u>: for from the first day that thou didst set thine heart to understand, and to chasten thyself before thy God, thy words were heard, and I am come for thy words.*

*¹³ <u>But the prince of the kingdom of Persia withstood me one and twenty days</u>: but, lo, <u>Michael, one of the chief princes, came to help me</u>; and I remained there with the kings of Persia.* (Underline mine)

Daniel commenced 3 weeks fast in verse 2, and in verse 12 above an angel, *likely* to be Gabriel came to him to let him know that God has already answered his prayers from day one and as he was coming to deliver his package to him the devil, prince of Persia withstood him for 21 days. The angel called for a backup and Archangel Michael came to help him. That's how they defeated the devil, prince of Persia.

## How to conquer evil spirits

*Matthew 11:12*

*And from the days of John the Baptist until now the kingdom of heaven suffereth violence, and the violent take it by force.*

Evil spirits are wicked, harmful, and deadly. However, as Christians, we are overcomers and more than conquerors in Jesus' name. It is important for a Christian to be *prepared in advance* against evil spirits in the following ways:

*Warfare prayers* – you need to enter into serious warfare prayer and fasting to violently take by force any package the devil is hijacking. If you have a prayer partner, ask them to support you.

You can see Gabriel asked Michael to help him. When a criminal is overpowering a police officer, they ask for a backup.

*Gift of discerning of spirits* - 1 Corinthians 12:10. This is the same as the gift to perceive things. You must depend on the Holy Spirit for this gift to be activated to enable you discern and deal with evil spirits and circumstances effectively. When this gift is in operation through the inspiration of the Holy Spirit, you will be able to see and hear things happening in the realm of the Spirit, and then take appropriate action.

## Psalms 92:10

*But my horn shalt thou exalt like the horn of an unicorn: I shall be anointed with fresh oil.*

## Psalms 144:1

*Blessed be the LORD my strength, which teacheth my hands to war, and my fingers to fight:*

During this warfare time, you have to ask God to exalt your horn like the horn of a unicorn and anoint you with fresh oil. Also ask Him to teach your hands and fingers to fight. Now I am writing metaphorically, Moses' horn was his rod. David's horn was his sling and five stones. Daniel's horn was prayer and fasting. What is yours? Strengthen it and use it against evil spirits. Bear in mind:

## 2 Corinthians 10:4

*(For the weapons of our warfare are not carnal, but mighty through God to the pulling down of strong holds;)*

*Sacrifice* – that will cost you can effectively end the works of the devil. Quality sacrifice has the capacity to miraculously overturn and end the bombardments of evil spirits, sicknesses, diseases, bondages, and oppression. After King David made a sacrifice in the scripture below, the plague ceased. The Bible says in:

## 2 Samuel 24:25

*And David built there an altar unto the LORD, and offered burnt offerings and peace offerings. So the LORD was intreated for the land, and the plague was stayed from Israel.*

Live a holy life - 1 Peter 1:16. Avoid sin - Romans 6:23. Always sharpen yourself spiritually by praying in tongues, and fasting, doing Bible study, meditation, praise and worship, and obedient to the Word of God. Use the name of Jesus by faith. Always believe you are an overcomer, and more than a conqueror in Jesus' name. Amen!

## PRAYER FOR YOU

I declare an end to all afflictions, infirmities, sicknesses, diseases, and oppressions of the devil in Jesus' name. The Bible says in:

## Psalms 34:19

*Many are the afflictions of the righteous: but the LORD delivereth him out of them all.*

## Isaiah 10:27

*And it shall come to pass in that day, that his burden shall be taken away from off thy shoulder, and his yoke from off thy neck, and the yoke shall be destroyed because of the anointing.*

*John 8:36 - If the Son therefore shall make you free, ye shall be free indeed.*

*Luke 21:13 - And it shall turn to you for a testimony.*

This is your time of victory and glory, and nothing will stop it in Jesus' name. Amen!

## ANGELS

Angels are heavenly supernatural bodies or entities. We have celestial bodies, cherubim, and seraphim. They are principally ministering spirits. However, we also see in the Bible that they manifest in the form of a person like we see in angel Gabriel and Archangel Michael.

### Angels are ministering spirits

*Hebrews 1:7*

*And of the angels he saith, <u>Who maketh his angels spirits</u>, and his ministers a flame of fire.* (Underline mine)

The scripture above tells us that angels are spirits.

*Hebrews 1:13-14*

*¹³ But to which of the <u>angels</u> said he at any time, Sit on my right hand, until I make thine enemies thy footstool?*

*¹⁴ <u>Are they not all ministering spirits</u>, sent forth to minister <u>for</u> them who shall be heirs of salvation?* (Underline mine)

The scripture above further confirms that angels are ministering spirits for the saints of God. This *implies* that we are to send angels on an errand. God also sends angels on errands. For example, we see God sending angel Gabriel to Zacharias and Mary in Luke Chapter one regarding the conception of John and Jesus. You can see from this that angels interact with human beings. See also Rev. 1:1, and Daniel 10:10-13. Activate your angels by obeying and declaring the scriptures, and praying.

## Angels excel in strength and do the commandments of God – The Word of God

*Psalms 103:20*

*Bless the LORD, ye his angels, that excel in strength, that do his commandments, hearkening unto the voice of his word.*

The above scripture makes it clear that angels excel in strength, and they also hearken and perform the commandments of God. This simply means that angels are powerful, and when you send them on errand in line with the written Word of God, they hearken and do them. Start sending your angels on errands by declaring and confessing the Word of God. Note that they are not likely to hearken and do evil, corrupt, wicked messages.

*Isaiah 37:36*

*Then the <u>angel</u> of the LORD went forth, and smote in the camp of the Assyrians a <u>hundred and fourscore and five thousand</u>: and when they arose early in the morning, behold, they were all dead corpses.* (Underline mine)

The above scripture demonstrates the fact that angels excel in strength. One angel killed 185,000 Assyrian soldiers.

## Angels are our invisible bodyguards

*Psalms 91:11-12*

*[11] For he shall give his angels charge over thee, to keep thee in all thy ways.*

*[12] They shall bear thee up in their hands, lest thou dash thy foot against a stone.*

*Psalms 34:7*

*The angel of the LORD encampeth round about them that fear him, and delivereth them.*

*Hebrews 12:22*

*But ye are come unto mount Sion, and unto the city of the living God, the heavenly Jerusalem, and to an innumerable company of angels,*

The above scriptures confirms that we have bodyguard angels also known as guardian angels, although they are invisible. Just be conscious of their presence even though you can't see them.

## Is man higher than angels in hierarchy?

Yes, man is higher than angels in authority and hierarchy. We have already seen that they are our ministering spirits and we are to send them on an errand. They also act as bodyguards to us.

*Psalms 8:4-5*

*⁴ What is man, that thou art mindful of him?
and the son of man, that thou visitest him?*

*⁵ For thou hast made him <u>a little lower than the angels</u>,
and hast crowned him with glory and honour. (Underline mine)*

*Psalm 8:5 (New American Standard)*

*Yet You have made him <u>a little lower than God,</u> And You crown him with glory and majesty! (Underline mine)*

*Psalm 8:5 (New Living Translation)*

*Yet you made them only <u>a little lower than God</u> and crowned them with glory and honor. (Underline mine)*

In Psalm 8:5 above, I laid KJV, NAS, and NLT side by side. KJV does not appear to be right because man is not "*a little lower than the angels,"* as it stated, but man is rather, *"a little lower than God,"* as stated in NAS, and NLT above. RSV, AMPC, also recorded the same thing as NAS, and NLT. This goes to show that man is higher in hierarchy than angels. To further prove this point, let's look at one more scripture.

## 1 Corinthians 6:3

<u>*Know ye not that we shall judge angels*</u>*? how much more things that pertain to this life?* (Underline mine)

Apostle Paul asked a question in the above scripture which suggests that we, the saints of God will judge angels, and if we are to judge them, then it implies that we are higher than them in authority and hierarchy, because you can't judge anyone higher than you in authority. Can a Lawyer judge the Judge in the court? No! Why? The Judge is higher in authority and hierarchy. We have also seen earlier that we are to send angels on errands. They are also to serve us as bodyguards.

## Ecclesiastes 5:6 says,

*"Suffer not thy mouth to cause thy flesh to sin; neither say thou before the angel, that it was an error:.."* First, note that the angel in this passage acted *for* and not *to* the person who made the vow. Second, if angels act on our behalf regarding our vows without even asking them, and you don't have to say you made a mistake, then you might as well intentionally and willfully instruct your guardian angel to act on your behalf regarding whatsoever you desire. Angels are our messengers, therefore, send them on errands.

Genesis 1:26 further tells us that man was made in the image and likeness of God, but angels are not. All these points suggest that man is higher in authority and hierarchy than angels. I hereby rest my case.

## Is there a difference between Angel and angel?

*Exodus 23:20*

*Behold, I send an <u>Angel</u> before thee, to keep thee in the way, and to bring thee into the place which I have prepared.* (Underline mine)

*Exodus 32:34*

*Therefore now go, lead the people unto the place of which I have spoken unto thee: behold, mine <u>Angel</u> shall go before thee: nevertheless in the day when I visit I will visit their sin upon them.* (Underline mine)

The above two scriptures are the only places in the entire KJV where the word "Angel" is used instead of "angel". The NKJV and AMPC also recorded them as "Angel." The capital letter 'A' in the word "Angel" seems to suggest that it was our Lord Jesus Christ, even though this is OT that He led and protected the Israelites, and not an ordinary "angel" with letter 'a'.

## Do angels appear in the form of a person?

Yes. We have already seen above that angels are ministering spirits and invisible guardians. There is also scriptural evidence suggesting that angels can manifest in the form of a person. Let's look at a few examples.

## Old Testament

### Hagar

*Genesis 16:7-9*

[7] *<u>And the angel of the LORD</u> found her by a fountain of water in the wilderness, by the fountain in the way to Shur.*

[8] *<u>And he said, Hagar,</u> Sarai's maid, whence camest thou? and whither wilt thou go? <u>And she said,</u> I flee from the face of my mistress Sarai.*

*⁹ And the angel of the LORD said unto her, Return to thy mistress, and submit thyself under her hands.* (Underline mine)

The above scripture records a conversation between the angel of the LORD and Hagar. You can see the underlined statements the angel made to Hagar in verses 8 and 9 which suggests that this angel appeared in the form of a person.

## Lot

*Genesis 19:1-3*

*¹ And there came two angels to Sodom at even; and Lot sat in the gate of Sodom: and Lot seeing them rose up to meet them; and he bowed himself with his face toward the ground;*

*² And he said, Behold now, my lords, turn in, I pray you, into your servant's house, and tarry all night, and wash your feet, and ye shall rise up early, and go on your ways. And they said, Nay; but we will abide in the street all night.*

*³ And he pressed upon them greatly; and they turned in unto him, and entered into his house; and he made them a feast, and did bake unleavened bread, and they did eat.* (Underline mine)

You can see the underlined scriptures above stating that Lot met the two angels, saw and spoke with them, and they even ate. This clearly suggests that they manifested to Lot in the form of persons because spirits should not be visible or eat.

## New Testament

## Zacharias

*Luke 1:11-13*

*¹¹ And there appeared unto him an angel of the Lord standing on the right side of the altar of incense.*

¹² _And when Zacharias saw him_, he was troubled, and fear fell upon him.

¹³ _But the angel said unto him_, Fear not, Zacharias: for thy prayer is heard; and thy wife Elisabeth shall bear thee a son, and thou shalt call his name John. (Underline mine)

Again, you can see from the above underlined scriptures that the angel of the Lord appeared to Zacharias and was standing – Verse 11. It says again in verse 12, "*And when Zacharias saw him,*" And verse 13 says, "*But the angel said unto him.*" Can a spirit stand? Can you see a spirit with your physical eyes? Zacharias saw this angel standing with his physical eyes, and they both had a conversation. This therefore suggests that this angel is a person. He even has a name – *Gabriel*.

## Mary

*Luke 1:26-28*

²⁶ *And in the sixth month the* _angel Gabriel_ *was sent from God unto a city of Galilee, named Nazareth,*

²⁷ *To a virgin espoused to a man whose name was Joseph, of the house of David; and the virgin's name was* _Mary_.

²⁸ _And the angel came in unto her, and said_, *Hail, thou that art highly favoured, the Lord is with thee: blessed art thou among women.* (Underline mine)

You can see angel Gabriel manifesting again in person to Mary and having a discussion with her in the above scriptures which further confirms that angels do appear in person because Gabriel has now appeared to two people.

## Peter

*Acts 12:7-8*

*⁷ <u>And, behold, the angel</u> of the Lord came upon him, and a light shined in the prison: <u>and he smote Peter on the side, and raised him up, saying,</u> Arise up quickly. And his chains fell off from his hands.*

*⁸ <u>And the angel said unto him,</u> Gird thyself, and bind on thy sandals. And so he did. And he saith unto him, Cast thy garment about thee, and <u>follow me</u>.* (Underline mine)

You can see an angel manifesting in person to Peter and having a discussion with him in the above scriptures which further confirms that angels do appear in person. Pay attention to the underlined texts noting that the angel taped Peter, spoke to him, and said, "Follow me" indicating that he is visible to Peter and not a spirit.

## Angels are helpers

*Hebrews 13:1-2*

*¹ Let brotherly love continue.*

*² Be not forgetful to entertain strangers: for thereby some have entertained angels unawares.*

Lot entertained the two strangers who came close to his house. He spoke to them and offered to support them to be refreshed, eat, and accommodate them. This kind gesture saved him and his family from destruction that happened in Sodom and Gomorrah.

Have you had people coming to you to beg for money? The above scripture encourages us to help and support strangers and beggars because they may be angels. You know they are angels because they may disappear after you have helped them.

## PRAYER FOR YOU

I pray that uncountable angels of the Lord in partnership with the Holy Spirit will locate you and your family now and perpetually encamp you to preserve you in Jesus' name. The angels will continually perfect all that concerns your health, finance, education, career, business, marriage, and family, to make you an overcomer, and more than a conqueror in Jesus' name. Amen!

I release the angels of God to reach out to you now with your special package of favor, miracles, blessings, and testimonies. Long life and prosperity to you and your family, more wisdom and anointing for you all in Jesus' name. Amen!

# CHAPTER SIX

# THE SYMBOLS OF THE HOLY SPIRIT

The Holy Spirit is associated with different symbols and metaphors such as water, fire, oil, wind, wine, dove, cloud, aprons, handkerchiefs, communion, and born again Christians. We will discuss this further.

**Water**

*John 7:37-39*

*[37] In the last day, that great day of the feast, Jesus stood and cried, saying, If any man thirst, let him come unto me, and drink.*

*[38] He that believeth on me, as the scripture hath said, out of his belly shall flow rivers of living water.*

*[39] (But this spake he of the Spirit, which they that believe on him should receive: for the Holy Ghost was not yet given; because that Jesus was not yet glorified.)*

The above scripture tells us that Jesus invited anyone thirsty to come and drink water which will turn to be rivers of living water that will flow from the person. When He said this He meant the Holy Spirit which has not yet been given because Jesus was not yet glorified.

The rivers of living water Jesus spoke about is a figure of speech or a metaphor because water is not the Holy Ghost. We have already seen that from our earlier chapters.

Jesus went through a process as follows for Him to be glorified: birth or incarnation, death or remission, resurrection, ascension, and Pentecost. One school of thought says Jesus was glorified after resurrection (See John 20:22), but the other believes it was when the Holy Spirit manifested in full measure on the day of Pentecost – Acts 2:1-4.

## John 4:13-14

[13] *Jesus answered and said unto her, Whosoever drinketh of this water shall thirst again:*

[14] *But whosoever drinketh of the water that I shall give him shall never thirst; but the water that I shall give him shall be in him a well of water springing up into everlasting life.*

Jesus spoke metaphorically again to the Samaritan woman in the above scripture using water.

## John 3:5

*Jesus answered, Verily, verily, I say unto thee, Except a man be born of water and of the Spirit, he cannot enter into the kingdom of God.*

Jesus also spoke to Nicodemus in the scripture above figuratively using water as in the previous manner.

## 1 Corinthians 10:4

*And did all drink the same spiritual drink: for they drank of that spiritual Rock that followed them: and that Rock was Christ.*

In the above verse, Apostle Paul made reference to the water the Israelites drank as a symbol of spiritual rock. Water is not the Holy Spirit. Just a symbol. See also 1 Corinthians 12:13.

## Fire

*Acts 2:3*

*And there appeared unto them cloven tongues like as of fire, and it sat upon each of them.*

The above scripture tells us that cloven tongues like as of fire sat upon each of the 120 disciples who received the baptism of the Holy Ghost. However, the fire is not the Holy Ghost. Just a symbol.

*Matthew 3:11*

*I indeed baptize you with water unto repentance: but he that cometh after me is mightier than I, whose shoes I am not worthy to bear: he shall baptize you with the Holy Ghost, and with fire:*

*Hebrews 12:29 – For our God is a consuming fire.*

The fire mentioned in the above scriptures is symbolic of the Holy Ghost. Fire is not the Holy Spirit.

## Oil

Oil is not the Holy Spirit but it has been used symbolically in different ways which we will look at now. For example, oil is used as anointing to empower a person for a certain task or position, like king, priest, judge, or prophet. Ordination and consecration.

## David

*Psalms 89:20*

*I have found David my servant; with my holy oil have I anointed him:*

## 1 Samuel 16:13

*Then Samuel took the horn of oil, and anointed him in the midst of his brethren: and the Spirit of the LORD came upon David from that day forward. So Samuel rose up, and went to Ramah.*

Anointing oil is a symbol of the Holy Spirit. Anointing makes things easy. In the first verse above, God said, He anointed David with His Holy oil suggesting the Holy Spirit. In the next verse above, Samuel also anointed David with oil. This anointing oil is used in ordination to confirm, and establish a person for a certain office.

## Saul

## 1 Samuel 10:1

*Then Samuel took a vial of oil, and poured it upon his head, and kissed him, and said, Is it not because the LORD hath anointed thee to be captain over his inheritance?*

Samuel also anointed Saul to be King of Israel. The anointing oil helps to empower a person, but it is only symbolic of the Holy Spirit.

## Anointing the sick

## James 5:14

*Is any sick among you? let him call for the elders of the church; and let them pray over him, anointing him with oil in the name of the Lord:*

We see James in the above verse saying the elders of a church should anoint a sick person with anointing oil. The church and the body of Christ needs to use this anointing oil. Note that before the anointing oil is used prayer is made to infuse the oil with the power of the Holy Spirit. But even at that, the oil is still symbolic.

### Wind

*Acts 2:2*

*And suddenly there came a sound from heaven as of a rushing mighty wind, and it filled all the house where they were sitting.*

*John 3:8*

*The wind bloweth where it listeth, and thou hearest the sound thereof, but canst not tell whence it cometh, and whither it goeth: so is every one that is born of the Spirit.*

Before the 120 disciples in the upper room were filled with the Holy Spirit, there was a rushing mighty wind, but this was not the Holy Spirit as some people suppose. The wind is only symbolic.

### Wine

*Ephesians 5:18*

*And be not drunk with wine, wherein is excess; but be filled with the Spirit;*

Apostle Paul says in the above scripture that we should not drink wine and be intoxicated because wine is a mocker. Instead we should be filled with the Holy Spirit because the Holy Spirit is of God, and by far better for a Christian because when the Holy Spirit fills somebody up they will be stirred up to do exploits and supernatural things. Hallelujah! Again, the wine is just a symbol of the Holy Spirit.

### Dove

*Matthew 3:16*

*And Jesus, when he was baptized, went up straightway out of the water: and, lo, the heavens were opened unto him, and he saw the Spirit of God descending like a dove, and lighting upon him:*

The dove expressed in the above verse seen by Jesus after baptism is a symbol of the Holy Spirit. The dove is a gentle bird, and the Holy Spirit is also gentle, peaceful, and loving. Jesus saw the Spirit of God descending *like* a dove, but not a dove.

## Pillar of cloud and fire to give them light

*Exodus 13:21*

*And the LORD went before them by day in a pillar of a cloud, to lead them the way; and by night in a pillar of fire, to give them light; to go by day and night:*

The scripture above says the LORD led the Israelites in a pillar of cloud by day, and pillar of fire by night. The cloud and fire are symbols of the Holy Spirit.

## Mediums – Handkerchiefs and aprons

*Acts 19:11-12*

*[11] And God wrought special miracles by the hands of Paul:*

*[12] So that from his body were brought unto the sick handkerchiefs or aprons, and the diseases departed from them, and the evil spirits went out of them.*

The above scripture tells us that Apostle Paul blessed handkerchiefs and aprons and it was infused with the power of God, and sent them out to sick people and diseases and evil spirits left sick people miraculously. The handkerchiefs and aprons served as mediums or symbols for spiritual transfer.

## Medium – Holy Communion

*1 Corinthians 10:16*

*The cup of blessing which we bless, is it not the communion of the blood of Christ? The bread which we break, is it not the communion of the body of Christ?*

The Holy communion we take is prayed on to infuse the power of God in it. That's why when we take it with the consciousness that it is indeed the body and the blood of Jesus, people are healed and receive all kinds of miracles. Communion is a very effective tool used in the church of God and the body of Christ. However, the communion is only a medium or symbol of the Holy Spirit.

## Born again Holy Spirit filled Christians

*1 Corinthians 6:19*

*What? know ye not that your body is the temple of the Holy Ghost which is in you, which ye have of God, and ye are not your own?*

*Acts 8:17*

*Then laid they their hands on them, and they received the Holy Ghost.*

Is a born again Spirit filled believer Holy Spirit? Absolutely not! But he is a living symbol of the Holy Spirit in the sense that his body is the temple of the Holy Spirit as stated in the above scripture.

Evangelist Philip finished a very successful crusade in the city of Samaria, and many received salvation and were baptized. Then Apostles Peter and John came from Jerusalem down to Samaria and laid hands on the new converts and they received the Holy Spirit as recorded in the above scripture. Through laying of hands, there was a transfer of the Holy Spirit. Apostle Paul also laid hands on about 12 new converts in Acts 19:6 and they were filled with the Holy Spirit and prophesied. We saw earlier that the handkerchiefs and aprons which passed through Paul's body also produced miracles, healings, and deliverances to people.

When some Men of God are ministering, you will see people falling down under the influence of the anointing of the Holy Spirit. This happens because they are carriers of the Holy Spirit. As a born again Spirit filled Christian, when you enter a place the atmosphere should also change. Does this make you the Holy Spirit? No! However, it's an indication that you are a living symbol or medium of the Holy Spirit.

# CHAPTER SEVEN

# SALVATION AND INDWELLING OF THE HOLY SPIRIT

The key to receive salvation, new birth, born again, regeneration, recreation, conversion, is to confess that Jesus Christ is your Lord and Saviour, and believe in your heart that God raised Him from the dead. You repent and forsake all sin. This is a standard salvation *pattern*. The process of salvation starts with a conviction by the Holy Spirit to the person to *surrender*.

Everybody was born into this world as a sinner. And this sin needs to be taken care of through the action of salvation by receiving Jesus Christ as your Lord and Saviour and be delivered by His blood which is for the *remission* of sin. Not *atonement*. Note that remission and atonement are sometimes used *interchangeably* but they are not synonyms, neither are they the same.

**Remission** has to do with total *cancellation* of a debt, charge, or penalty. That's what Jesus did for mankind with His own life for the sin He did not commit. Jesus paid the price for our sins with His blood on the cross of Calvary *once* and that's remission. Total cleansing of sin. Jesus Himself said in:

Matthew 26:28

*For this is my blood of the new testament, which is shed for many for the <u>remission</u> of sins.* (Underline mine)

This is what Apostle Peter said about Jesus in the two scriptures below:

## Acts 2:38

<u>Then Peter said unto them</u>, Repent, and be baptized every one of you in the name of Jesus Christ for the <u>remission</u> of sins, and ye shall receive the gift of the Holy Ghost. (Underline mine)

## Acts 10:43

To him give all the prophets witness, that through his name whosoever believeth in him shall receive <u>remission</u> of sins. (Underline mine)

The writer of Hebrews made it very clear that Jesus died *once* for the remission of our sin.

## Hebrews 9:26-28

26 For then must he often have suffered since the foundation of the world: but now <u>once</u> in the end of the world hath he appeared to put away sin by the sacrifice of himself.

27 And as it is appointed unto men <u>once</u> to die, but after this the judgment:

28 So Christ was <u>once</u> offered to bear the sins of many; and unto them that look for him shall he appear the second time without sin unto salvation. (Underline mine)

## Hebrews 10:10-14

10 By the which will we are sanctified through the offering of the body of Jesus Christ <u>once</u> for all.

11 And every priest standeth daily ministering and offering oftentimes the same sacrifices, which can never take away sins:

*¹² But this man, after he had offered <u>one</u> sacrifice for sins for ever, sat down on the right hand of God;*

*¹³ From henceforth expecting till his enemies be made his footstool.*

*¹⁴ For by <u>one</u> offering he hath perfected for ever them that are sanctified.* (Underline mine)

The underlined *once* and *one* in the above scriptures shows that Jesus died once to save mankind as a substitutionary sacrifice for their sins. The fact that the word remission appeared 10 times in the New Testament of the KJV, and none in the Old Testament is a further proof that remission is what Jesus did and only once.

**Atonement** is *amending*, propitiation, appeasing, restitution, reparation, recompense, redress of sin which the high priests did in the Old Testament yearly by making sacrifices with the blood of bulls, bullocks, goats in the holy of holies. I have already mentioned this in Chapter four. Atonement is Old Testament yearly sacrifice thing, and the writer of Hebrews put it beautifully like this:

## Hebrews 10:1-4

*¹ For the law having a shadow of good things to come, and not the very image of the things, can never with those <u>sacrifices which they offered year by year continually</u> make the comers thereunto perfect.*

*² For then would they not have ceased to be offered? because that the worshippers once purged should have had no more conscience of sins.*

*³ But in those <u>sacrifices</u> there is a remembrance again <u>made of sins every year</u>.*

*⁴ <u>For it is not possible that the blood of bulls and of goats should take away sins.</u>* (Underline mine)

Can you see from the above scripture that the high priest made sacrifices with the blood of bulls every year for the *atonement* of sin in the Old Testament? The word atonement appeared in KJV of the Old Testament 69 times, and just once in the New Testament. This goes to show that atonement is clearly an Old Testament yearly sacrifice thing. In *conclusion*, did Jesus die for the *remission* of our sins? YES! Did Jesus die for the *atonement* of our sins? NO! The blood of bulls were offered in the Old Testament yearly by the high priest for the atonement of sins.

## Everybody was born into this world as a sinner.

This is how King David put it in:

*Psalms 51:5*

*Behold, I was shapen in iniquity; and in sin did my mother conceive me.*

This sinful nature was inherited from the first Adam when he committed sin by disobeying the instruction of God not to eat the forbidden fruit. God commanded Adam thus in:

*Genesis 2:17*

*But of the tree of the knowledge of good and evil, thou shalt not eat of it: for in the day that thou eatest thereof thou shalt surely die.*

The serpent deceived Adam and Eve and they ate this fruit and died spiritually. Originally, God created man to have fellowship with him – *Koinonia*[7]. The Bible says in:

*Isaiah 43:21*

*This people have I formed for myself; they shall shew forth my praise.*

However, man's act of disobedience to sin broke this fellowship as he was sent out of the Garden of Eden. The Bible says in:

## Genesis 3:24

*So he drove out the man; and he placed at the east of the garden of Eden Cherubims, and a flaming sword which turned every way, to keep the way of the tree of life.*

God detests sin. And there was a disconnection between God and man because of this serious sin, but God wants to fix it. The Bible says in:

## Romans 6:23

*For the wages of sin is death; but the gift of God is eternal life through Jesus Christ our Lord.*

## Romans 3:23

*For all have sinned, and come short of the glory of God;*

## Romans 5:12

*Wherefore, as by one man sin entered into the world, and death by sin; and so death passed upon all men, for that all have sinned:*

## Jesus Christ our Saviour

In order for man to be restored back to God, God had to send His only begotten Son to die as a substitutionary sacrifice for the sins of the whole world. Jesus had to die to reconcile man back to God.

## John 3:16-18

[16] *For God so loved the world, that he gave his only begotten Son, that whosoever believeth in him should not perish, but have everlasting life.*

[17] For God sent not his Son into the world to condemn the world; but that the world through him might be saved.

[18] He that believeth on him is not condemned: but he that believeth not is condemned already, because he hath not believed in the name of the only begotten Son of God.

## Colossians 1:14

In whom we have redemption through his blood, even the forgiveness of sins:

## 2 Corinthians 5:21

For he hath made him to be sin for us, who knew no sin; that we might be made the righteousness of God in him.

## 1 Peter 3:18

For Christ also hath once suffered for sins, the just for the unjust, that he might bring us to God, being put to death in the flesh, but quickened by the Spirit:

## John 1:29

The next day John seeth Jesus coming unto him, and saith, Behold the Lamb of God, which taketh away the sin of the world.

## Romans 4:25

Who was delivered for our offences, and was raised again for our justification.

## Isaiah 53:5

But he was wounded for our transgressions, he was bruised for our iniquities: the chastisement of our peace was upon him; and with his stripes we are healed.

*1 Timothy 2:5*

*For there is one God, and one mediator between God and men, the man Christ Jesus;*

Jesus Christ acted as the Access Bridge, and mediator to restore us back to God by His substitutionary death for our sin on the cross of Calvary.

## Salvation

The Holy Spirit is the One that convicts people to give their life to Jesus. The Holy Spirit will crack, and break down even the most hardened people with stony hearts, and they will receive salvation.

*John 16:8*

*And when he is come, he will reprove the world of sin, and of righteousness, and of judgment:*

*Ephesians 2:8-9*

*8 For by grace are ye saved through faith; and that not of yourselves: it is the gift of God:*

*9 Not of works, lest any man should boast.*

## The standard pattern for salvation

A confession based on the scripture below has to be made:

*Romans 10:9-10*

*9 That if thou shalt confess with thy mouth the Lord Jesus, and shalt believe in thine heart that God hath raised him from the dead, thou shalt be saved.*

*¹⁰ For with the heart man believeth unto righteousness; and with the mouth confession is made unto salvation.*

Once a person confesses by faith with their mouth that Jesus Christ is now their personal Lord and Saviour, and believe in their heart that God raised Him from the dead, he becomes a born again Christian with regenerated spirit. The Holy Spirit moves in and interacts with the human spirit to activate it and also to indwell the new convert. This whole exercise is a mystery and a miracle.

Let me give you a simple analogy as I try to explain this. When a woman is pregnant with a baby, the internal organs and senses of the baby become fully developed in the womb by 9 months ready to be born. None of the organs and senses will function in the womb freely the way they will start functioning after birth in a new environment. But as soon as the baby is born, the organs and senses are activated and they begin to function normally in the new environment. For example, the baby starts to see, hear, breath, sleep, eat, cry, laugh etc because he has been regenerated into a new environment, for example, born as a citizen of the United Kingdom.

Similarly, the human organs and senses of an atheist, unbeliever is spiritually dead because of the sin of Adam. But once he receives salvation, Christ dwells in him, and the Holy Spirit moves in to interact with his human spirit, this action activates the organs and senses of this person, and they become a born again Christian with regenerated spirit into a new environment, to become a citizen of the Kingdom of God. Hallelujah!

## Salvation prayer

I hereby confess with my mouth that henceforth Jesus Christ is my personal Lord and Saviour. I believe in my heart that God raised Him from the dead. I renounce and repent of my sins. Lord have mercy on me. Thank you for saving me in Jesus' name. Amen!

Congratulations my Friend. You are now born again. Go on and celebrate it.

## Proof of salvation.

Sometimes people are born again but they are not sure if they are or not. They want some sort of sign or proof. Many years ago, there was this young boy in church who comes out each time a Minister of God makes an altar call for people to receive salvation. He has done this over 10 times. So one day an altar call was made and he stood up to come out but the ushers intervened and tried to stop him but he refused.

USHER: Salvation is a one-time thing but you have come out more than10 times before. Please go back.

YOUNG BOY: No! I don't want to go to hell. I have to do it again today just to make sure at least one of them will get me into heaven.

USHERS: They started laughing, and left him to go again.

Now, this young boy is probably scared of going to hell as he said. But has he been serious with all the previous confessions he made? Perhaps he has not been making the confessions by faith, and therefore in doubt. Or he is probably having fun with the confessions. Be serious with salvation prayer. Do it by faith. No jokes.

Once an atheist, or an unbeliever confesses the name of Jesus Christ that becomes a litmus test that he has accepted Jesus as his Lord and Saviour. Some people give their life to Jesus but are not sure because they are expecting some kind of experience. Note that the basic things you need to do is believe, confess by faith, repent, and then there could be a feeling of peace and joy.

## 1 Corinthians 12:3

*Wherefore I give you to understand, that no man speaking by the Spirit of God calleth Jesus accursed: and that no man can say that Jesus is the Lord, but by the Holy Ghost.*

## Romans 10:13

*For whosoever shall call upon the name of the Lord shall be saved.*

## 1 John 5:10-12

*10 He that believeth on the Son of God hath the witness in himself: he that believeth not God hath made him a liar; because he believeth not the record that God gave of his Son.*

*11 And this is the record, that God hath given to us eternal life, and this life is in his Son.*

*12 He that hath the Son hath life; and he that hath not the Son of God hath not life.*

## John 5:24

*Verily, verily, I say unto you, He that heareth my word, and believeth on him that sent me, hath everlasting life, and shall not come into condemnation; but is passed from death unto life.*

## 2 Corinthians 5:17-19

*17 Therefore if any man be in Christ, he is a new creature: old things are passed away; behold, all things are become new.*

*18 And all things are of God, who hath reconciled us to himself by Jesus Christ, and hath given to us the ministry of reconciliation;*

¹⁹ *To wit, that God was in Christ, reconciling the world unto himself, not imputing their trespasses unto them; and hath committed unto us the word of reconciliation.*

## Romans 5:19

*For as by one man's disobedience many were made sinners, so by the obedience of one shall many be made righteous.*

## 1 Corinthians 15:45

*And so it is written, The first man Adam was made a living soul; the last Adam was made a quickening spirit.*

## Salvation is a mystery and miracle of the Lord, by the Word and the Holy Spirit

The miracle of salvation is one performed by the joint operation of the confession of the Word of God and the power of the Holy Spirit. There is inseparable fusion between the human spirit and the Holy Spirit in the process of salvation or conversion. Think of the analogy of marriage where two people become one when they get married. The new birth experience is similar. The new covert is joined to Christ to become one. There is an interaction, a fusion, that joins both and it is a mystery and a miracle. The Bible says in:

## 1 Corinthians 6:16-17

*16. What? know ye not that he which is joined to an harlot is one body? for two, saith he, shall be one flesh.*

*17. But he that is joined unto the Lord is one spirit.*

## Romans 8:9

*But ye are not in the flesh, but in the Spirit, if so be that the Spirit of God dwell in you. Now if any man have not the Spirit of Christ, he is none of his.*

## Ezekiel 36:26-27

²⁶ *A new heart also will I give you, and a new spirit will I put within you: and I will take away the stony heart out of your flesh, and I will give you an heart of flesh.*

²⁷ *And I will put my spirit within you, and cause you to walk in my statutes, and ye shall keep my judgments, and do them.*

At this point, after the unbeliever has proclaimed that Jesus Christ is his personal Lord and Saviour, the Adamic sinful nature dies, and he effectively becomes a new creature in Christ Jesus. A born again Christian. Congratulations!

## 2 Corinthians 5:17

*Therefore if any man be in Christ, he is a new creature: old things are passed away; behold, all things are become new.*

## Galatians 2:20

*I am crucified with Christ: nevertheless I live; yet not I, but Christ liveth in me: and the life which I now live in the flesh I live by the faith of the Son of God, who loved me, and gave himself for me.*

When an unbeliever, atheist, natural man declares that Jesus is now his Lord and Saviour, his spirit becomes regenerated or recreated with the activation of indwelling of the Holy Spirit which will grant him eternal life. This process happens instantly as the declaration is made by faith. Salvation is a now thing. You don't postpone it.

## 2 Corinthians 6:2

*(For he saith, I have heard thee in a time accepted, and in the day of salvation have I succoured thee: behold, now is the accepted time; behold, now is the day of salvation.)*

## Examples of indwelling of the Holy Spirit in a believer

Let's look at two examples to demonstrate indwelling of the Holy Spirit in a believer.

### Acts 8:12

*But when they <u>believed Philip preaching</u> the things concerning the kingdom of God, and the name of Jesus Christ, <u>they were baptized, both men and women</u>.* (Underline mine)

Evangelist Philip was in the city of Samaria to preach in a crusade, and miracles, healings, and deliverances happened. The above scripture gives an indication that they received salvation because they believed Philip's preaching, and that's why they were baptized. This scenario clearly demonstrates that they had indwelling of the Holy Spirit with the encounter they had. To further confirm this, we see that Apostles Peter and John later came down from Jerusalem and prayed and laid hands on these new converts and they received infilling of the Holy Spirit. Read Acts 8:14-17 below:

### Acts 8:14-17

*14 Now when the apostles which were at Jerusalem heard that Samaria had received the word of God, they sent unto them <u>Peter and John</u>:*

*15 Who, when they were come down, <u>prayed for them, that they might receive the Holy Ghost:</u>*

*16 <u>(For as yet he was fallen upon none of them: only they were baptized in the name of the Lord Jesus.)</u>*

*17 <u>Then laid they their hands on them, and they received the Holy Ghost</u>.* (Underline mine)

**NOTE:** *Some Christians receive salvation with indwelling of the Holy Spirit and stop there. They don't bother about further growth. They are permanently stagnated at this level. That's why they don't speak in tongues. This should not be so. After indwelling of the Holy Spirit, you must seek for the infilling of the Holy Spirit, and then the power of the Holy Spirit. Why? The path of the just is like the shining light that must shine more and more unto the perfect day. No dimming! It has to shine brighter and brighter, from one level of glory to a higher level of glory. Hallelujah!*

## John 20:19-22

*¹⁹ Then the same day at evening, being the first day of the week, when the doors were shut where the disciples were assembled for fear of the Jews, came <u>Jesus</u> and stood in the midst, and saith unto them, Peace be unto you.*

*²⁰ And when he had so said, <u>he shewed unto them his hands and his side. Then were the disciples glad, when they saw the Lord.</u>*

*²¹ Then said Jesus to them again, Peace be unto you: as my Father hath sent me, even so send I you.*

*²² And when he had said this, he breathed on them, and saith unto them, <u>Receive ye the Holy Ghost:</u>* (Underline mine)

The above scenario presents Jesus' first appearance to the disciples after resurrection. They saw Him and believed that God has raised Him from the dead in line with Romans 10:9-10 which is the standard pattern of salvation. They also received indwelling of the Holy Spirit when Jesus said in verse 22, "*...Receive ye the Holy Ghost:*" They later received *infilling* of the Holy Ghost and spoke in *tongues* on the day of Pentecost in Acts 2:1-4.

## You must be born again to enter heaven

One day a hardened criminal walked into a church, and the preacher made an altar call for people to come forward and receive salvation in order to be able to enter heaven. This criminal said to himself, "That's simple. I will do it now to guarantee my place in heaven, and afterwards I will go back to my old ways." Is this repentance? No!

**Repentance** means sincere regret or remorse for one's sin or wrongdoing, and also make a U-turn from the sin. You renounce your sins. This means making a commitment not to repeat the sin. If you go back to the sin, you have not truly repented.

## Mark 13:13

*And ye shall be hated of all men for my name's sake: but he that shall endure unto the end, the same shall be saved.*

The above scripture tells us that he that keeps up with his salvation until the end or rapture shall be saved indeed. You can't claim to receive salvation, and still hold on to your worldly rascally lifestyle. That's totally unacceptable. When you give your life to Jesus you become a heavenly citizen, a royal priesthood, and ambassador of Christ, and you have to step up to the standards of this Kingdom in character, and in all you do.

## John 3:3-7

*Jesus answered and said unto him, Verily, verily, I say unto thee, <u>Except a man be born again, he cannot see the kingdom of God.</u>*

*⁴ Nicodemus saith unto him, How can a man be born when he is old? can he enter the second time into his mother's womb, and be born?*

*⁵ Jesus answered, Verily, verily, I say unto thee, <u>Except a man be born of water and of the Spirit, he cannot enter into the kingdom of God.</u>*

6. *That which is born of the flesh is flesh; and that which is born of the Spirit is spirit.*

7. *Marvel not that I said unto thee, <u>Ye must be born again</u>.* (Underline mine)

According to Master Jesus Christ in the above scriptures, the basic non-negotiable condition everybody *must* satisfy before they can *enter* the Kingdom of God is that they *must be born again of water and the Spirit*, otherwise they can't even *see* it. He concluded by saying in verse 7, "...*Ye must be born again.*" If you are not born again, I urge you to obey the words of Jesus and do so now.

## Water baptism

Baptism is a total immersion or submersion (not sprinkling or pouring) in water by a person. The Greek word for "Baptism" is *Baptisma*[8] as a noun, and *Baptizo*[9] as a verb. This act symbolizes the death, burial, and resurrection with our Lord Jesus Christ, and also marks an end of all sin as a significance.

There is no particular order that water baptism should be done. For example, it can be done after salvation, indwelling of the Holy Spirit, or after baptism of the Holy Spirit. The main thing is that it should be done by a born again Christian because Jesus commanded that all believers *must* do it. Jesus said in:

### Matthew 28:19

*Go ye therefore, and teach all nations, <u>baptizing</u> them in the name of the Father, and of the Son, and of the Holy Ghost:* (Underline mine)

Jesus is not a hypocrite. What He commanded us to do, He also did in:

### Matthew 3:16

*<u>And Jesus, when he was baptized</u>, went up straightway out of the water: and, lo, the heavens were opened unto him, and he saw <u>the</u>*

<u>*Spirit of God descending like a dove, and lighting upon him*</u>: (Underline mine)

The above scripture tells us that Jesus was baptized and filled with the Holy Spirit.

## Acts 2:38

*Then <u>Peter said</u> unto them, <u>Repent</u>, and be <u>baptized</u> every one of you in the name of Jesus Christ for the <u>remission</u> of sins, and ye shall receive the gift of the <u>Holy Ghost</u>.* (Underline mine)

*Apostle Peter gave us in the above underlined scripture a procedure unbelievers should follow to be admitted into the Kingdom of God. He said, they should repent, be baptized in the name of Jesus for the remission of sins, and then receive the gift of the Holy Ghost. The church and the body of Christ needs to follow this biblical pattern.*

## Romans 6:3

*Know ye not, that so many of us as were baptized into Jesus Christ were baptized into his death?*

## 1 Corinthians 12:13

*For by one Spirit are we all baptized into one body, whether we be Jews or Gentiles, whether we be bond or free; and have been all made to drink into one Spirit.*

The scriptures tell us that when a person is born again by confessing that Jesus is now their Lord and Saviour, they also need to have water baptism by total immersion.

In addition to water baptism, the new convert needs the infilling of the Holy Spirit which is usually characterised by the evidence of speaking in tongues.

## After salvation, what next?

A lot of people receive salvation and then stop there. No! After you have received salvation, you must embark on a deliberate, intentional programme that will help you to keep growing as a Christian. You must not be stagnated. You must desire and expect to grow. The Bible says in:

### 1 Peter 2:2

*As newborn babes, desire the sincere milk of the word, that ye may grow thereby:*

There has to be a methodical approach to your growth process. What I have here is a suggestion, but I believe it will be helpful. Start doing the following after salvation.

1. Be filled with the Holy Spirit, and start speaking with tongues.
2. Learn how to pray effectively – in tongues and with scriptures.
3. Start studying the Bible to renew your mind.
4. Start fellowshipping with other believers in a good church and join a department to serve in the vineyard of the Lord.
5. Aim to discover your purpose in life. You need to discover your vision, dream, or assignment in life. This can be discovered through the Word of God, your passion, interests, and even challenges you've been through.
6. Through your Bible study, begin to learn basic doctrines, biblical principles and how to apply them in your life. These include prayer, fasting, Holy Spirit, angels, health, holiness, giving, prosperity, integrity, humility, evangelism, relationships, marriage etc.
7. You have to keep reading Christian books, listen regularly to teachings and preaching of good Ministers of God on different subjects. This will help you to develop and grow from a babe in Christ to a mature Christian.

# CHAPTER EIGHT

# INFILLING OF THE HOLY SPIRIT

When a person receives salvation, they become a born again Christian, and have a regenerated or recreated spirit, and the Holy Spirit indwells the person. The person gets water baptism. The next thing that needs to be done is Infilling of the Holy Spirit also called baptism of the Holy Spirit, and this usually happens with the evidence of speaking with tongues.

*Acts 2:4*

*And they were all <u>filled with the Holy Ghost</u>, and began to <u>speak with other tongues</u>, as the Spirit gave them utterance.* (Underline mine)

The above scripture is an account of about 120 disciples in the upper room on the day of Pentecost who received infilling of the Holy Spirit and spoke with tongues. Speaking with tongues is usually the clear evidence that a born again Christian is filled with the Holy Spirit.

*Acts 19:6*

<u>*And when Paul had laid his hands upon them, the Holy Ghost came on them; and they spake with tongues, and prophesied.*</u> (Underline mine)

The above is the scenario that happened in Ephesus between Apostle Paul and about 12 disciples. They were baptized in the name of John, but Paul told them it's not so. He ministered to them and baptized them in the name of Jesus. Paul laid hands on them, they were filled with the Holy Ghost, spoke with tongues, and prophesied.

## Acts 10:44-47

**44** <u>While Peter yet spake these words, the Holy Ghost fell on all them which heard the word.</u>

**45** And they of the circumcision which believed were astonished, as many as came with Peter, because that on the Gentiles also was poured out the gift of the Holy Ghost.

**46** <u>For they heard them speak with tongues</u>, and magnify God. Then answered Peter,

**47** Can any man forbid water, that these should not be <u>baptized</u>, which have received the Holy Ghost as well as we? (Underline mine)

The above scenario is an account of what happened to Cornelius and his household. The Holy Ghost fell on all of them as Apostle Peter preached, and they spoke with tongues, and were baptized in water. It's interesting to note that Cornelius and his household received both the *indwelling* and *infilling* of the Holy Ghost at the same time. That was why they were able to speak with *tongues* straightaway. Double portion of the anointing of the Holy Spirit was received. Praise God!

## Tongues

As we have already seen, tongues is the language of the Holy Ghost which a believer speaks when they are filled with the Holy Spirit. Tongues in Greek means *Glossa*[10], and speaking in tongues is *Glossolalia*. The Bible says in:

## 1 Corinthians 14:2

*For he that speaketh in an unknown tongue speaketh not unto men, but unto God: for no man understandeth him; howbeit in the spirit he speaketh mysteries.*

I was born in Nigeria, from the Igbo tribe, and I speak Igbo language fluently. When I speak Igbo, nobody can dispute that I am not from the Igbo tribe.

I migrated to the United Kingdom where English is their first language. Before I naturalized and became a UK citizen, I had to do a Trinity College London "Secure English Language Test" and "Life in the UK" test. These examinations, among other things, are to test the candidate's ability in English Language, cultures, and traditions of United Kingdom. I passed the tests and I was granted United Kingdom citizenship. Can you see that even an earthly kingdom considers it important for you to speak their language before they will grant you citizenship? I speak English fluently, and I write as well. When I speak English nobody will ever dispute that I am not a citizen of the United Kingdom.

When I gave my life to Jesus, my spirit became regenerated, and my Lord Jesus Christ dwelt in me, with indwelling of the Holy Spirit. I became a born again citizen of the Kingdom of God. I started reading my Bible in order to know the cultures, traditions, and principles of the Kingdom of God. When I had infilling of the Holy Spirit, I started speaking the heavenly language called *tongues*. Today, when I speak in tongues, nobody can dispute that I am not born again, heavenly citizen. I speak it fluently. Even the devil knows that I am a true citizen of the Kingdom of God because I bombard, blast, destroy his works, and deceive him uncountable times as I speak the mysteries called praying in the Spirit or tongues. I am proud of this my heavenly Father's language.

As a United Kingdom parent, when you have a new born baby and they grow to be about one year six months and they don't speak English language, will you be concerned or not? I think it will become a concern for the parents. They will seek to know why the child does not speak English, and perhaps begin to teach the child or hire a teacher to do so. Is it not a sign of stagnation when the situation persists?

Similarly, when a person becomes a born again Christian, and for a long time they are not able to speak the Kingdom of God language, tongues, it should also be a concern. To this I will suggest the person should meet an anointed Holy Spirit filled Man of God operating in that dimension to minister to them to receive the baptism of the Holy Spirit and start speaking in tongues. Alternatively, ask God to fill you up with the Holy Spirit so that you will speak with tongues. The Bible says in:

## Luke 11:13

*If ye then, being evil, know how to give good gifts unto your children: how much more shall your heavenly Father give the Holy Spirit to them that ask him?*

Speaking the language of your tribe, nation, or kingdom will always be an advantage and a means of easy identification. Language also serves as a tool to connect with people emotionally, build a rapport, and promote love, peace, and unity. As good as your native language, or English language may appear to be, they are earthly languages and by far inferior to heavenly citizen language called tongues. This language is superior to all languages on earth. It's a language for those who desire supernatural power.

To prove that all earthly languages are inferior to heavenly tongues, read Genesis 11:1-9 and see what happened. Verse 1 says, *"And the whole earth was of one language, and of one speech."* They decided to build a city and tower that will reach heaven. God was concerned. To stop them, He simply confounded or changed their language – verse 7. After their language was confounded, the project stopped and they were scattered – verse 9. This was earthly language. You can see there is no earthly language God cannot change. Tongue is a heavenly language. Will God stop His own language?

Are you born again into the Kingdom of God? Do you now speak the heavenly language called tongues? Assuming an English person is in the midst of Germans, French, or Spanish people speaking their language, do you think that person will be comfortable and be able to integrate well? Don't you think the English person will feel alienated? But if they all speak English together the atmosphere will change and become more friendly, lively, and lovely. That's the power of language.

The man who wrote about speaking in tongues in the Bible, Apostle Paul said this about tongues in 1 Corinthians 14:5 & 39. "...I would that ye all spake with tongues..." And, "...forbid not to speak with tongues..." And then He said again in:

## 1 Corinthians 14:18

*I thank my God, I speak with tongues more than ye all:*

Apostle Paul is not a hypocrite. He wrote in his 1 Corinthians Chapter 14 epistle that believers should speak in tongues. And in the above scripture, he says he speaks in tongues more than the whole Corinthians congregation church. Meaning, you can't beat me in this tongue, it is good, I value it, and it edifies me. He says again in:

## 1 Corinthians 11:1

*Be ye followers of me, even as I also am of Christ.*

The great Apostle and Christian mentor says in the above scripture follow me. Meaning we are to copy, and do the things we see him do including speaking in tongues because he is of Christ. How about that?

I believe Jesus Christ, our Christian model must have spoken in tongues. The Bible did not expressly state that He did, but it is implied He did. There is an indication He must have done so. He said in:

### Mark 16:17

*And these signs shall follow them that believe; In my name shall they cast out devils; <u>they shall speak with new tongues</u>;* (Underline mine)

Again, Jesus is not a hypocrite. He will never tell you to do what He doesn't do. He said one of the signs that will follow believers is that, *"...they shall speak with new tongues;"* This statement suggests that Jesus prayed in tongues.

## Some benefits of praying in tongues

As a Christian who truly desires to keep growing, and keep doing exploits, then praying or speaking in the language of the Holy Ghost is necessary.

Let's look at some of the benefits of praying in tongues.

1. When you pray in tongues, you can pray for a longer period of time. You will be able to have a good prayer exercise.
2. When you pray in tongues, you are communicating with God, and not men. See 1 Corinthians 14:1.
3. When you pray in tongues, you are edifying yourself. To edify is to teach yourself in a way that will improve your mind or character. See 1 Corinthians 14:4 & 26.
4. When you pray in tongues, you are speaking mysteries, and unknowingly praying for things you are not even aware of. Mystery language unveils mysterious things. 1 Corinthians 14:2.
5. Praying or speaking in tongues will profit you more when you are able to interpret. Therefore, desire to also interpret the tongues you speak. See 1 Corinthians 14:13&27. When you interpret your tongues, you will have an understanding of what God is saying, and what to do.
6. When I pray in an unknown tongue my spirit prayeth, but my understanding is unfruitful. Praying in tongues will launch

you into the spiritual realm. Hallelujah! See 1 Corinthians 14:14.
7. To pray in tongues will build you up in the most holy faith. You will be charged up like a battery. *Jude 1:20* says, *"But ye, beloved, building up yourselves on your most holy faith, praying in the Holy Ghost,"*
8. To pray in tongues will strengthen you with might.

## *Ephesians 3:16*

*That he would grant you, according to the riches of his glory, to be strengthened with might by his Spirit in the inner man;*

## *Ephesians 6:18*

*Praying always with all prayer and supplication in the Spirit, and watching thereunto with all perseverance and supplication for all saints;*

9. Praying or speaking in tongues is a heavenly language that confuses and destroys the works of the devil.
10. To pray in tongues will help sharpen you, and cause you to be filled with the Holy Ghost.

## *Ephesians 5:18-19*

[18] *And be not drunk with wine, wherein is excess; but be filled with the Spirit;*

[19] *Speaking to yourselves in psalms and hymns and spiritual songs, singing and making melody in your heart to the Lord;*

## **Continuous infilling of the Holy Spirit**

It is also important to note that we are to be continually filled with the Holy Spirit in order to be very effective Christians. For example, Apostle Peter was filled with the Holy Spirit in Acts 2:4, 4:8, and 4:31.

## Ephesians 5:18

*And be not drunk with wine, wherein is excess; but be filled with the Spirit;*

The statement, *"...but be filled with the Spirit;"* suggests that a Christian's infilling should be continuous. It should not be a one-time thing.

## Ephesians 3:19

*And to know the love of Christ, which passeth knowledge, that ye might be filled with all the fulness of God.*

We are to be continuously filled with the Holy Spirit, and with all the fullness of God. Apostle Peter was filled three times with the Holy Spirit as an *individual*. We also see that a *family* can be filled with the Holy Spirit. We saw that Cornelius and his household were filled with the Holy Spirit in Acts 10:44 earlier. Zacharias, his wife Elisabeth, and their son John were all also filled with the Holy Spirit in Luke 1:15, 41, and 67 respectively as a family. We have already seen that the entire 120 disciples of the *church* in Jerusalem were filled with the Holy Spirit in Acts 2:4.

# CHAPTER NINE

# THE HOLY SPIRIT EMPOWERMENT

Empowerment simply means to give a person power or authority to do something. It also means to give ability and enablement to a person or thing. After a new convert receives salvation and indwelling of the Holy Spirit, they move up by being filled with the Holy Spirit, with evidence of speaking with tongues. The next level is that they have to move up through spiritual growth to be endued with power which will enable them to start doing more signs, wonders, miracles, and exploits for the kingdom of God.

As Christians, our Lord Jesus will always be our model and pattern of operation. Let's look at the process Jesus had to go through before he was empowered by the Holy Ghost.

Before our Lord Jesus Christ was anointed with Holy Ghost power, He had to pay the price, and went through the process as follows: He was conceived by the power of the Holy Spirit – Luke 1:35; He was filled with the Holy Spirit immediately after water baptism – Matthew 3:16-17, Luke 3:21-22; led by the Holy Spirit into the wilderness in isolation to be tempted for 40 days while He fasted – Luke 4:1-2. Afterwards, the Bible says in:

*Luke 4:14*

*And Jesus returned in the power of the Spirit into Galilee: and there went out a fame of him through all the region round about.*

## Acts 10:38

*How God anointed Jesus of Nazareth with the Holy Ghost and with power: who went about doing good, and healing all that were oppressed of the devil; for God was with him.*

This is the biblical pattern for acquiring supernatural Holy Ghost power. Therefore, if you desire this power, pay the price, go through the process, and you will be endued with power.

## Luke 24:49

*And, behold, I send the promise of my Father upon you: but tarry ye in the city of Jerusalem, until ye be endued with power from on high.*

## Acts 1:8

*But ye shall receive power, after that the Holy Ghost is come upon you: and ye shall be witnesses unto me both in Jerusalem, and in all Judaea, and in Samaria, and unto the uttermost part of the earth.*

## Luke 10:19

*Behold, I give unto you power to tread on serpents and scorpions, and over all the power of the enemy: and nothing shall by any means hurt you.*

## 1 Corinthians 4:20

*For the kingdom of God is not in word, but in power.*

We must not be powerless Christians who only talk, but we must have the ability to demonstrate the power of God in Jesus' name. Amen! Let's look at a scenario where the disciples of Jesus couldn't perform. They failed to cure a sick child. Power and authority needs to be activated!

## Matthew 17:14-21

*¹⁴ And when they were come to the multitude, <u>there came to him a certain man</u>, kneeling down to him, and saying,*

*¹⁵ <u>Lord, have mercy on my son: for he is lunatick</u>, and sore vexed: for ofttimes he falleth into the fire, and oft into the water.*

*¹⁶ <u>And I brought him to thy disciples, and they could not cure him</u>.*

*¹⁷ Then Jesus answered and said, O faithless and perverse generation, how long shall I be with you? how long shall I suffer you? bring him hither to me.*

*¹⁸ <u>And Jesus rebuked the devil; and he departed out of him: and the child was cured from that very hour</u>.*

*¹⁹ <u>Then came the disciples to Jesus apart, and said, Why could not we cast him out</u>?*

*²⁰ And Jesus said unto them, Because of your <u>unbelief</u>: for verily I say unto you, If ye have <u>faith</u> as a grain of mustard seed, ye shall say unto this mountain, Remove hence to yonder place; and it shall remove; and nothing shall be impossible unto you.*

*²¹ <u>Howbeit this kind goeth not out but by prayer and fasting</u>.* (Underline mine)

A certain man brought his lunatic son to the disciples of Jesus in the above scenario but they could not cure the boy. However, verse 18 tells us that, *"And Jesus rebuked the devil; and he departed out of him: and the child was cured from that very hour."* The disciples of Jesus became concerned and asked Jesus in verse 19, *"Then came the disciples to Jesus apart, and said, Why could not we cast him out?"* Verse 20-21 above gives the answer. Unbelief, lack of faith, prayer and fasting is the reason, says Jesus. In summary – no power! Jesus has been for

40 days training, fasting and praying, tested by the devil and He destroyed him by quoting scriptures three times "It is written" in the wilderness. Afterwards, He was empowered by the Holy Ghost. So He cast out the devil oppressing the boy and cured him. The disciples have not been through this process. So they don't have the capacity to cast out devils. Power and authority needs to be activated!

Now I am writing respectfully and metaphorically as I give this illustration. This is to give you a picture of the process a person has to go through to be empowered. The process is as follows:

*Holy Ghost Primary School* – Here, you obtain a certificate of salvation, indwelling of the Holy Spirit, and water baptism with ease – See Ephesians 2:8-9.

*Holy Ghost Secondary School* – Here, you achieve a certificate of infilling of the Holy Spirit, with speaking in tongues evidence perhaps with a little effort of tarrying – See Luke 24:49 and Acts 1:4.

*Holy Ghost University* – To obtain a degree in Holy Ghost Power which will enable you to start doing more signs, wonders, miracles, and exploits for the kingdom of God, you have to go through a training process in *isolation* like Jesus for 40 days, 3 years, or whatever as prescribed by the Master. *There is a price to pay here*, but it is worth it because after graduation, you will be able to cast out the devil oppressing the lunatic boy, and cure him, plus many other supernatural things. Power and authority is activated during your Holy Ghost University isolation degree programme!

## Isolation: Some reasons for God's isolation and the experiences

## What is isolation?

Isolation is simply a period of separation, seclusion, solitariness, confinement, and being alone to face training, trials, tests, and encounter God.

# THREE TYPES OF ISOLATION

## 1. Self isolation

This happens when you are fed up with the things happening in your life, and you desire a change, a higher next level, and you personally make a sincere, serious decision to isolate yourself and go through spiritual exercises to encounter God and be blessed.

*Jacob* is a good example of someone who isolated himself and encountered God. The Bible says in:

Genesis 32:22-26

22. And he rose up that night, and took his two wives, and his two womenservants, and his eleven sons, and passed over the ford Jabbok.

23. And he took them, and sent them over the brook, and sent over that he had.

24. <u>And Jacob was left alone; and there wrestled a man with him until the breaking of the day.</u>

25. And when he saw that he prevailed not against him, he touched the hollow of his thigh; and the hollow of Jacob's thigh was out of joint, as he wrestled with him.

26. And he said, Let me go, for the day breaketh. And he said, <u>I will not let thee go, except thou bless me</u>. (Underline mine)

When you are self isolating, you have the absolute liberty to dictate your own terms and conditions under which to carry out your desired isolation. You make your own rules, and you can decide to also keep or break the rules. Jacob isolated himself from his family and was alone. You need to discipline yourself well enough to be able to have an encounter with God when you are in self isolation.

Isolate yourself like an eagle on a mountain, and come out refreshed and soaring much better. Interestingly, everyone is eligible to choose whether to self-isolate or not.

## 2. God instructs you to isolate

This happens when God gives you instruction to isolate yourself. Everyone is a potential candidate to be asked by God to go into isolation. So get ready because you could be next online. However, if God asks you to be isolated, you may choose to obey or not to obey Him, and He is likely to respect your choice.

*Abraham* is a good example of someone God instructed to isolate himself and he obeyed. The Bible says in:

*Genesis 12:1-2*

1. <u>Now the LORD had said unto Abram, Get thee out of thy country, and from thy kindred, and from thy father's house, unto a land that I will shew thee</u>:

2. *And I will make of thee a great nation, and I will bless thee, and make thy name great; and thou shalt be a blessing:* (Underline mine)

When God instructs you to isolate, the exercise will be based on His terms and conditions, except you decide to disobey His instructions, but that cannot be helpful. It's better to obey and benefit from the isolation. Abraham obeyed God and was blessed.

## 3. The Holy Spirit leads/drives or draws/pulls you into isolation

This is the highest form of isolation. This happens when a person is led or drawn by the Holy Spirit into isolation. This happens unannounced, unexpectedly, and it is mandatory because the Holy

Spirit is invisible and irresistible. You are arrested into isolation and you simply don't have a choice.

***Jesus*** is a good example of someone led/driven by the Spirit into isolation.

## *Matthew 4:1*

*Then was Jesus led up of the spirit into the wilderness to be tempted of the devil.*

## *Mark 1:12*

*And immediately the spirit driveth him into the wilderness.*

This is the kind of isolation that will certainly make God anoint you with the Holy Ghost and with power. It's a *pattern*. To be eligible to be drawn by the Holy Spirit to be tested, and given further training by God, you are likely to have walked with God for some time. Jesus was prepared for 30 years before He was led by the Spirit into isolation to be tested.

When you are led or drawn by the Spirit into isolation, you do not have the liberty to dictate your own terms and conditions. God will make the rules, and if you decide to break the rules, that will count as disobedience, and that will make you repeat tests and training, and this is likely to prolong your isolation period.

## Duration of isolation

Isolation period varies from one individual to another, and it also depends on the purpose or assignment God wants you to accomplish. It could be one day, 7 days, 21 days, 40 days, 3 years, 7 years, 13 years, 21 years, 40 years etc. Isolation can be temporary or lengthy. For example, the Bible says in:

## Mark 1:35

*And in the morning, rising up a great while before day, he went out, and departed into a solitary place, and there prayed.*

## Luke 6:12

*And it came to pass in those days, that he went out into a mountain to pray, and continued all night in prayer to God.*

Jesus isolated himself temporarily in the morning, and all night to pray as shown in the above two scriptures. However, Jesus was also in isolation in the wilderness for 40 days before His ministry started - Mathew 4:1-2; Elijah for 40 days - 1 Kings 19:8; and Moses for 40 days - Exodus 34:28.

A person's entire period of training and preparation to become a Man of God, Kingdom Financier, Politician, etc can also count as an isolation period. For example, Moses was 40 years old when God called him. He was Isolated and trained for 40 years before his ministry started at the age of 80 years. Joseph had his dream at the age of 17, but became the Prime Minister of Egypt after 13 years training in isolation at the age of 30. The same thing happened to King David. Scholars believe he was 17 years when he was anointed to be the king of Israel. But he was enthroned at the age of 30 after 13 years training in isolation. Jesus was trained for 30 years.

In the secular world, people spend years in School to be trained for a chosen career. For example, to get a PhD could take about 6+5+5+2+3=21 years. That's how God will also spend years training anyone He has chosen in different phases. And the standard of God is superior to the worldly standard.

When you are in isolation going through God's training, your life may seem to be put on hold or even retrogressing. However, after the training in isolation, God will catapult you to be in front and also be the head with overwhelming blessings. Miracles upon miracles, and blessings upon blessings starts happening after a successful isolation training period. Why? Because God has approved you to enter into a new season and higher realm of glory.

## Things to experience during isolation

Isolation process comes in phases as planned by God, and He will take you into deeper and deeper dimensions, to achieve more intimacy.

One of the things God will do to simulate a wilderness scenario is that He will gradually ensure everything is taken from you. Yes, everything! He will ensure you lose your Job, cut you off from family and friends relationships. Stop your car, and ensure all other home appliances like your fridge, cooker, washing machine, hoover, microwave etc breakdown. He will create artificial Cave Adullum in your home. Or create artificial wilderness of Engidi, Maon, Ziph, Paran, Ziklag etc in your home.

Your job or income will be stopped. This means you will be unable to buy food, or pay your bills. No electricity, heating, hot water etc. It's kind of a weird situation. Your finances will drift into the negatives, which is red or debt. However, don't panic. Just chill because it's only temporary. After a while, when your soul starts prospering, your finances will start to also grow positively. But prior to that, you and your finances will go through the valley of the shadow of death. Your finances will look like this: -50, -22, -5, 0, 5, 30, 100, 500, 2,000, 7,000 etc.

Your toys will be stopped or taken away from you. Your mobile phone toy, internet access, social media access, TV etc will all be stopped! Yes, they will all be gradually stopped! Why? God is a very jealous God and does not want anything or anybody to distract your attention from focusing on Him alone while you are in isolation. Besides, He wants you to develop 100% trust in Him, and not in any man or thing. *(I am not a prophet of doom, and I am not writing fiction. This is a true picture I am painting of God's isolation, wilderness, and cave training experience for Holy Ghost empowerment.)*

If you still have access to all your toys, everything, and everybody, then you are self isolating and you have chosen to do what you like. And nothing is likely to come out of such unserious isolation. Did Jacob, Abraham, and Jesus take their mobile phone, TV, internet, social media, car etc. with them into isolation? They didn't. This means that when you are instructed by God to isolate or drawn by the Spirit into isolation then God will definitely ensure you have a good taste of the wilderness experience right there in your home by taking everything from you. All He needs to do to achieve this is to press one button. That is, stop all your money. But don't panic because He will restore it back in abundance after the isolation and training.

The only reason why a person's isolation training programme is not likely to be as stringent, as tough, and as long as I am describing in this book is probably because the person's assignment is not on a large scale. The bigger your assignment, the tougher and longer your training programme will be. For example, you can be called to a geographical area or a people as a Man of God. Has God called you to a city, locality, state, nation, nations, continent, or globally? If you are called to a city, your isolation period may just be, for example, one month. Do you sincerely think the training programme for somebody called to a continent will also be one month isolation? Never! It will be far tougher and longer. That is God for you. The standard of God is very high. Is the training period and curriculum for a Primary school teacher, and a University professor going to be the same? Of course not!

## Isolation: Some reasons for God's isolation and the experiences

**1. *Communication*:** God will isolate you to create a quiet atmosphere to speak to you. God loves privacy and confidentiality. So when your attention is needed, He will isolate you.

For example, if God wants to disclose your vision, dream, purpose, or assignment to you, He will isolate you, or ask you to isolate yourself. Another example of when God will isolate you is to give you direction and guidance, plus strategies for your assignment. He told Moses while alone to build the tabernacle according to the pattern He showed him in:

*Exodus 25:40*

*And look that thou make them after their pattern, which was shewed thee in the mount.*

Note that God may not speak to you audibly. He uses different methods to communicate. Therefore, you must pay attention to perceive and discern when God speaks to you.

**2. *Love*:** God will isolate you because He loves you, and because you are different, unique, precious, and His favourite. You are the chosen one.

*Romans 9:13, "As it is written, Jacob have I loved, but Esau have I hated."*

*Matthew 22:14, "For many are called, but few are chosen."*

**3. *Intimacy*:** God will ask you to isolate in order to promote intimacy with you. This is a time you will engage in very serious spiritual exercises including Bible study, meditation, prayers, praise, worship, fasting etc. This will help create a conduit for intimate relationships with God.

## 1 Timothy 4:8

*For bodily exercise profiteth little: but godliness is profitable unto all things, having promise of the life that now is, and of that which is to come.*

## Philippians 3:10

*That I may know him, and the power of his resurrection, and the fellowship of his sufferings, being made conformable unto his death;*

## Daniel 11:32

*And such as do wickedly against the covenant shall he corrupt by flatteries: but the people that do know their God shall be strong, and do exploits.*

Spiritual exercise will lead to godliness for you to know God more. The more you get to know God, His nature, and Modus operandi through deliberate enthusiastic spiritual exercises, the better. This will take you into deeper dimensions where you will truly begin to feel the literal presence, glory, and peace of God because you have tarried in His presence for a long time.

You will be filled with the Holy Spirit, peace, joy, and wisdom of God as you have a very deep intimate relationship with God. This is a fantastic experience you will love.

**4. *Pruning*:** God will isolate you to prune you so that you can bear much fruit. This can be a very painful exercise, but it is truly worth it when it is completed.

## John 15:2

*Every branch in me that beareth not fruit he taketh away: and every branch that beareth fruit, he purgeth it, that it may bring forth more fruit.*

Pruning will involve pain as God cuts off bad habits, bad character, bad relationships etc. God will also prune vices such as anger, bitterness, lust, greed, covetousness, hatred, unforgiveness, malice, envy, jealousy, pride, ego, foolishness etc.

The pain of pruning is similar to surgery done by a doctor to remove a tumour, cataract, appendicitis, pile etc. Painful process but afterwards the patient will be free, well and healthy. A Horticulturist pruning plants and flowers will make it grow better. Squeezing orange for juice brings out the taste. And olive fruits for olive oil.

**5. Purging and refinement**: God will isolate you to purge, purify, and refine you to become a vessel of honour fit for the master's use.

## Malachi 3:3

*And he shall sit as a refiner and purifier of silver: and he shall purify the sons of Levi, and purge them as gold and silver, that they may offer unto the LORD an offering in righteousness.*

The Goldsmith and silversmith will pass gold and silver through fire to refine it. That's how God will shake you up, disrupt your plans, and superimpose His own plans for you as a master planner.

In Daniel Chapter 3, Shadrach, Meshach, and Abednego were thrown into a fiery furnace by King Nebuchadnezzar for not bowing down to his golden image god. Jesus appeared in the fire to ensure they were not hurt. When they came out, they were promoted by the same King Nebuchadnezzar that threw them into fire. *Daniel 3:30* says, *"Then the king promoted Shadrach, Meshach, and Abednego, in the province of Babylon."* Go through the isolation trials knowing that you are not alone, and you will come out a better person, and be promoted. God has great plans for you.

## Jeremiah 29:11

*For I know the thoughts that I think toward you, saith the LORD, thoughts of peace, and not of evil, to give you an expected end.*

## Proverbs 19:21

*There are many devices in a man's heart; nevertheless the counsel of the LORD, that shall stand.*

You must be willing to surrender yourself to undergo the isolation process by paying the price to become a godly person with integrity.

**6. Chastisement**: God will isolate you to discipline you to become a better Christian. He is doing this because He loves you. Chastisement is not punishment. Endure the process as a good soldier of Christ.

## Revelation 3:19

*As many as I love, I rebuke and chasten: be zealous therefore, and repent.*

## Hebrews 12:11

*Now no chastening for the present seemeth to be joyous, but grievous: nevertheless afterward it yieldeth the peaceable fruit of righteousness unto them which are exercised thereby.*

## Job 23:10

*But he knoweth the way that I take: when he hath tried me, I shall come forth as gold.*

As you are isolated by God to be chastised, it will appear to be like a punishment but it's not. Afterwards, you will become beautiful and glorious.

**7. Vessel of honour**: God will isolate you because He wants to transform you to become a vessel of honour to be used for a special purpose. See it as a privilege.

## 2 Timothy 2:20-21

[20] *But in a great house there are not only vessels of gold and of silver, but also of wood and of earth; and some to honour, and some to dishonour.*

[21] *If a man therefore purge himself from these, he shall be a vessel unto honour, sanctified, and meet for the master's use, and prepared unto every good work.*

God is preparing you for promotion and elevation during periods of isolation. Therefore, be patient and endure the process as a good soldier of Christ.

**8. To grow up**: God will instruct you to isolate in order to stir you to grow up. For example, you have been a born again Christian for many years but you are still a baby regarding spiritual exercises like Bible study, prayers, praise, worship and fasting. God can instruct you to isolate to get you to learn to do it because He has a better and bigger assignment for you.

## 1 Peter 2:2

*As newborn babes, desire the sincere milk of the word, that ye may grow thereby:*

## Hebrews 5:12-14

[12] *For when for the time ye ought to be teachers, ye have need that one teach you again which be the first principles of the oracles of God; and are become such as have need of milk, and not of strong meat.*

¹³ *For every one that useth milk is unskilful in the word of righteousness: for he is a babe.*

¹⁴ *But strong meat belongeth to them that are of full age, even those who by reason of use have their senses exercised to discern both good and evil.*

God can isolate you so that you can intentionally, and deliberately engage in meaningful Bible study, meditation, prayers, praise, worship, and fasting that will enable you to grow. Note that the Bible study will greatly enhance a renewed mind-set. - Romans 12:2.

## 1 Corinthians 13:11

*When I was a child, I spake as a child, I understood as a child, I thought as a child: but when I became a man, I put away childish things.*

God will instruct you to isolate so that you can give up childish things hindering you from growing up as a Christian. God will prune and strip you internally and externally of everything ungodly, unhealthy, junks, and weights hindering your growth. God wants you to grow up!

Anyone who is not willing to go through the process of isolation may end up being stagnated. The choice is yours.

**9. *Healing*:** God can instruct a person to isolate to heal them. God is a specialist in healing physical and emotional wounds. He also heals people from wrong mentality, bad habits and character. Therefore, He will isolate you to grant holistic healing to you. This includes deliverance from the mentality of business failure, financial failure, career challenges, relationship challenges and failure, and get you to start soaring like an eagle.

*Psalms 147:3 - He healeth the broken in heart, and bindeth up their wounds.*

**10. Fear dies**: God will isolate you so that you can be built up. He will get you to confront and kill those things that scare you. He will present things like fear of poverty, sickness, and failure in life to you to crush them. He will get you to kill your Goliath while in isolation. You will come out of isolation fearing nothing. You will not be a coward again. You will be as bold as a lion.

*2 Timothy 1:7*

*For God hath not given us the spirit of fear; but of power, and of love, and of a sound mind.*

**11. Trust**: One of the things God is out to establish in your life while in isolation is the ability to always look up unto Him as your source. That's why He took everything from you. That's one of the ways He uses to say, trust me and not men. No matter how tough things may appear to be during your isolation period, your daily bread is guaranteed. He can still provide manna from heaven for His beloved. So relax and trust God.

*Psalms 118:8 - It is better to trust in the LORD than to put confidence in man.*

*Proverbs 3:5*

*Trust in the LORD with all thine heart; and lean not unto thine own understanding.*

*Jeremiah 17:7*

*Blessed is the man that trusteth in the LORD, and whose hope the LORD is.*

*Jeremiah 17:5*

*Thus saith the LORD; Cursed be the man that trusteth in man, and maketh flesh his arm, and whose heart departeth from the LORD.*

Note that God will test you while in isolation till He is satisfied you can be trusted with the anointing, power, money, information, promotion etc. God will find out if He can trust you with Holy Ghost power. Some people abuse the Holy Ghost power given to them by God. So you will face trials and tests. In Acts 8:18-20, Simon the sorcerer offered Apostle Peter and John money to get Holy Ghost power, but Apostle Peter told him off. This kind of man is likely to misuse Holy Ghost power. Don't you think so?

**12. Metamorphosis**: Transformation, and evolvement, takes place as you isolate yourself. You will feed yourself greatly with the Word of God in order to have a renewed mind. This will enable you to detach from the worldly lifestyle. You will die daily to bad habits, vices, and bad character. Apostle Paul says in 1 Cor. 15:31, *"....I die daily."* The Bible says in:

## Galatians 2:20

*I am crucified with Christ: nevertheless I live; yet not I, but Christ liveth in me: and the life which I now live in the flesh I live by the faith of the Son of God, who loved me, and gave himself for me.*

Philippians 1:21, *"For to me to live is Christ, and to die is gain."*

## John 12:24

*Verily, verily, I say unto you, Except a corn of wheat fall into the ground and die, it abideth alone: but if it die, it bringeth forth much fruit.*

## Matthew 16:25

*For whosoever will save his life shall lose it: and whosoever will lose his life for my sake shall find it.*

*Luke 14:33*

*So likewise, whosoever he be of you that forsaketh not all that he hath, he cannot be my disciple.*

A butterfly metamorphosis goes through different stages from egg to larva, pupa, caterpillar, and then to butterfly. You will go through a process in the isolation cocoon. This is how God will transform you beyond recognition to evolve into a more glorious supernatural version to do signs, wonders, miracles and attracting the blessings of God. Hallelujah! You will begin to soar like an eagle because you have stepped into a more superior dimension of you. Praise God!

**13. Signs indicating the isolation period is coming to an end:** After you've been through the tests, and training, an angel will visit you and minister to you. You will begin to see angelic signs like numbers in the form of 1111, 2222, 3333, 4444, 5555 etc, plenty of coins on the ground, feathers on the ground, rainbows in the sky etc. There will be synchronicities and serendipities happening to match your experiences. There could also be dreams and visions. All you've got to do is pay attention to the *patterns* and see how they match biblical patterns, life of patriarchs, autobiographies, and biographies you have read. These are positive signs of a victorious isolation period. There will also be restoration, and open new doors of blessings. You are now ready to commence your assignment.

**14. More wisdom and anointing:** When you successfully go through God's isolation, He will fill you with Holy Spirit power, wisdom, and anointing.

*Psalms 89:20*

*I have found David my servant; with my holy oil have I anointed him:*

*Proverbs 4:7*

*Wisdom is the principal thing; therefore get wisdom: and with all thy getting get understanding.*

When God gives you more wisdom, power, and anointing, you enter a higher realm to do exploits for the kingdom of God.

**15. *Alignment and power:*** When you satisfactorily go through God's isolation, He will empower and approve you as you align yourself with Him, our Lord Jesus, and the Holy Spirt - trinity. You truly become a god because you have God's consciousness always. God is love and you have aligned yourself with love, operating at the same energy, vibration, and frequency level. God created us in His own image and likeness.

*Psalms 82:6*

*I have said, Ye are gods; and all of you are children of the most High.*

At this point,

You honour and fear God more

You are filled with the Holy Spirit, love, compassion, peace, joy, and humility

You stay true to your godly values

You start having more encounters and experiential knowledge of God

You begin to do more exploits for the kingdom of God

*Acts 1:8*

*But ye shall receive power, after that the Holy Ghost is come upon you: and ye shall be witnesses unto me both in Jerusalem, and in all Judaea, and in Samaria, and unto the uttermost part of the earth.*

*John 14:12*

*Verily, verily, I say unto you, He that believeth on me, the works that I do shall he do also; and greater works than these shall he do; because I go unto my Father.*

**16. Gratitude**: You will become a person of gratitude, thanksgiving, and worship unto God. You are always grateful to God for all the things He does for you. You adopt a lifestyle of praise.

*1 Thessalonians 5:18*

*In every thing give thanks: for this is the will of God in Christ Jesus concerning you.*

God will also give you a Holy Spirit inspired song to sing, dance, and celebrate.

*Psalms 40:3*

*And he hath put a new song in my mouth, even praise unto our God: many shall see it, and fear, and shall trust in the LORD.*

## THE ANOINTING OF THE HOLY SPIRIT EMPOWERMENT

Before God will anoint a person with the Holy Spirit power, he must go through a training and test process. The anointing of the Holy Spirit is not cheap. The process involves many things, which includes the following:

### Sacrifice

When people hear the word sacrifice, they immediately think of giving tithes and offerings. However, the sacrifice you will make in this process will involve you giving your all or emptying your bank account again and again until God is satisfied you are no longer materialistic and that you will always honour Him above money, and all other things. No more idols.

## Matthew 6:24

*No man can serve two masters: for either he will hate the one, and love the other; or else he will hold to the one, and despise the other. Ye cannot serve God and mammon.*

God will test you again and again with money and other material things to know if your heart is more focussed on Him than money and material things. Your goal is to ensure that you keep passing the tests until money and other material things will no longer mean anything to you. You love God above all things!

God is a jealous God, and therefore He will not allow money or any other thing to be a distraction from focusing on Him alone. *Ye cannot serve God and mammon* at the same time. Choose one!

In Genesis 22:1-2, God commanded Abraham to offer his son Isaac that he loves as a sacrifice. Tough one! Are you prepared for this kind of sacrifice? In Mark 12:41-44, the poor widow gave her all as a sacrifice and Jesus noticed her. Can you give your all out of love to God and to promote the kingdom of God? In Genesis 4:4-5, Abel gave his best as offering and God had respect unto him, but had no respect for Cain and his offering. Make no mistake about this, sacrificial giving will always provoke the attention of God! When you make a sacrificial giving to God, it turns out to be an opportunity for a covenant. **Psalm 50:5** says, "*Gather my saints together unto me; those that have made a covenant with me by sacrifice.*"

## Romans 12:1-2

[1] *I beseech you therefore, brethren, by the mercies of God, that ye present your bodies a living sacrifice, holy, acceptable unto God, which is your reasonable service.*

*² And be not conformed to this world: but be ye transformed by the renewing of your mind, that ye may prove what is that good, and acceptable, and perfect, will of God.*

Note that your giving and sacrifice will get to the point where you have to present your own body as a living sacrifice. You have to become the ultimate sacrifice, and not your money and other things that you give to God. You will lay yourself down on the altar of God and be a living sacrifice unto God. This happens when you surrender all, and lay down your all for God. This happens when you enthrone, honour, and love God as your number one, and above all things, and everyone.

The songwriter **William McDowell** paints a good picture of what happens as he puts it beautifully in his song published in 2009:

### *I Give Myself Away*

*I give myself away*
*I give myself away*
*So You can use me*
*I give myself away*
*I give myself away*
*So You can use me*

*1:*
*Here I am*
*Here I stand*
*Lord, my life is in your hands*
*Lord, I'm longing to see*
*Your desires revealed in me*
*I give myself away*

*2:*
*Take my heart*
*Take my life*
*As a living sacrifice*
*All my dreams, all my plans*
*Lord I place them in your hands*

*I give myself away*
*I give myself away*
*So You can use me*
*I give myself away*
*I give myself away*
*So You can use me*

*I give myself away*
*I give myself away*
*So You can use me*

*I give myself away*
*I give myself away*
*So You can use me*
*Here I am to worship, here I am to bow down*
*Here I am to say that You're my God, You're altogether lovely, altogether worthy, altogether wonderful to me.*

*Bridge:*
*My life is not my own*
*To you I belong*
*I give myself, I give myself to You*
*I give myself away*
*I give myself away*
*So You can use me*

## John 12:24

*Verily, verily, I say unto you, Except a corn of wheat fall into the ground and die, it abideth alone: but if it die, it bringeth forth much fruit.*

## Galatians 2:20

*I am crucified with Christ: nevertheless I live; yet not I, but Christ liveth in me: and the life which I now live in the flesh I live by the faith of the Son of God, who loved me, and gave himself for me.*

## 1 Corinthians 15:31

*I protest by your rejoicing which I have in Christ Jesus our Lord, I die daily.*

## Luke 14:33

*So likewise, whosoever he be of you that forsaketh not all that he hath, he cannot be my disciple.*

This process will surely take you through the valley of the shadow of death where you will die to all ungodly things, and you will forsake all things and wholeheartedly embrace and ***align*** yourself with God. Note that to forsake all truly means to forsake all and that includes the things you consider to be very precious to you. When you have done this, you will truly belong to God wholeheartedly. God is a very jealous God – Exodus 34:14. His name is Jealous. He is more jealous than a partner in marriage who does not want anyone to even speak to or touch you. God is by far more jealous than man.

## Service

You must be actively involved in the activities that promote the kingdom of God. As a member of a local church, you have to join a department and actively engage in working in the vineyard of the Lord. For example, do evangelism to promote the kingdom of God and win souls. Give tithes, offerings, donations, alms to help the church, the poor and needy, and the vulnerable in the society. Do all you can to promote, support, and build the kingdom of God. Your acts of kindness and generosity must be motivated by the love of God, and not a mind-set of exchange or business with God.

## Colossians 3:23-24

[23] *And whatsoever ye do, do it heartily, as to the Lord, and not unto men;*

*24 Knowing that of the Lord ye shall receive the reward of the inheritance: for ye serve the Lord Christ.*

## Worldly Lifestyle

One of the things God will achieve through this process before anointing you is to ensure you get rid of worldly habits, and lifestyle. As you do this, you will deliberately, and intentionally begin to apply heavenly kingdom principles in your life.

### 1 John 2:15-17

*15 Love not the world, neither the things that are in the world. If any man love the world, the love of the Father is not in him.*

*16 For all that is in the world, the lust of the flesh, and the lust of the eyes, and the pride of life, is not of the Father, but is of the world.*

*17 And the world passeth away, and the lust thereof: but he that doeth the will of God abideth for ever.*

### Colossians 3:2

*Set your affection on things above, not on things on the earth.*

You must give up your worldly lifestyle and begin to operate by heavenly kingdom citizen's principles if you truly desire the anointing of the Holy Spirit empowerment.

## Holiness

God is holy, and we are to also be holy because we are created in the image and likeness of God. To be holy means to be *set apart* for a special divine purpose. As you isolate or set yourself apart, you must also be *devoted* to spiritual exercises such as Bible study, prayers, fasting, praise, and worship.

## Numbers 6:1-3

*¹ And the LORD spake unto Moses, saying,*

*² Speak unto the children of Israel, and say unto them, When either man or woman shall separate themselves to vow a vow of a Nazarite, to separate themselves unto the LORD:*

*³ He shall separate himself from wine and strong drink, and shall drink no vinegar of wine, or vinegar of strong drink, neither shall he drink any liquor of grapes, nor eat moist grapes, or dried.*

The above scripture tells us what people who separate or isolate themselves must do. True isolation comes with rules or Dos and Don'ts!

### Samson

In the Old Testament, Samson is a good example of someone who was set apart. Have you ever wondered why Samson was so powerful? Before he was born, an angel of the Lord appeared to the mother and said to her in:

## Judges 13:3-5

*³ And the angel of the LORD appeared unto the woman, and said unto her, Behold now, thou art barren, and bearest not: but thou shalt conceive, and bear a son.*

*⁴ Now therefore beware, I pray thee, and drink not wine nor strong drink, and eat not any unclean thing:*

*⁵ For, lo, thou shalt conceive, and bear a son; and no razor shall come on his head: for the child shall be a Nazarite unto God from the womb: and he shall begin to deliver Israel out of the hand of the Philistines.*

Do you want to be as powerful as Samson? Separate or set yourself apart. Drink no wine or strong drink, stop all bad habits, and all worldly lifestyle.

## John

In the New Testament, John is a good example of someone who was set apart. Have you ever wondered why John was Jesus' forerunner? Before he was born, an angel of the Lord appeared to the father and said to him in:

## Luke 1:15

*For he shall be great in the sight of the Lord, and shall drink neither wine nor strong drink; and he shall be filled with the Holy Ghost, even from his mother's womb.*

John was filled with the Holy Ghost even from his mother's womb. He did not drink wine, or strong drink. He was in isolation in the deserts until the time of his showing forth to Israel. Read the scripture below. What a price to pay for the Holy Ghost anointing and empowerment. John recognized Jesus, announced Him, and baptized Him.

## Luke 1:80

*And the child grew, and waxed strong in spirit, and was in the deserts till the day of his shewing unto Israel.*

## Integrity and Honesty

A person must demonstrate the quality of integrity and honesty to a good extent before God will empower him with the anointing of the Holy Spirit. You must be a disciplined person with good character.

God will test your integrity in certain areas such as idolatry, greed, sexual immorality, anger, envy, loyalty, hatred, bitterness, forgiveness, pride, lying, etc. You will get rid of all bad habits, worldly, and ungodly lifestyle.

*Psalm 25:21*

*Let integrity and uprightness preserve me; for I wait on thee.*

*Proverbs 11:3*

*The integrity of the upright shall guide them: but the perverseness of transgressors shall destroy them.*

**The heart condition**

One of the reasons why it will take a long time before God anoints a man with Holy Ghost power is that God will ensure the man is thoroughly broken, humble, and aligned with His purpose. The Bible says in:

*Jeremiah 17:9-10*

*[9] The heart is deceitful above all things, and desperately wicked: who can know it?*

*[10] I the LORD search the heart, I try the reins, even to give every man according to his ways, and according to the fruit of his doings.*

The above scripture tells us that the heart of man is desperately wicked. God will not give His anointing to such a person. Therefore, He will pass this person through a process. This will involve giving your life to Jesus to become a born again Christian, being filled with the Holy Spirit, and continuously feeding yourself with the Word of God in order to have a renewed mind, and have a pure heart.

The Bible says in:

## Psalms 51:17

*The sacrifices of God are a broken spirit: a broken and a contrite heart, O God, thou wilt not despise.*

This process will also involve brokenness especially of your heart. You will be broken to the point of detesting sin, remorse, repentance, and total surrender unto God. Then God will create in you a clean heart, and renew a right spirit within you.

## Proverbs 23:26

*My son, give me thine heart, and let thine eyes observe my ways.*

God will demand that you give Him your heart. If you don't give it to Him wholeheartedly, He will search and try your heart again and again until He is satisfied that you can be trusted and given the Holy Ghost empowerment anointing. The Bible says in:

## Jeremiah 17:10

*I the LORD search the heart, I try the reins, even to give every man according to his ways, and according to the fruit of his doings.*

King David says in:

## Psalm 139:23

*Search me, O God, and know my heart: try me, and know my thoughts:*

Can you be bold enough to give God the permission today to search your heart, and try you to know your thoughts? If you permit God, He will see all the skeletons in your cupboard if there is any because there's absolutely nothing you can hide from God.

Note that it will take a ***long time***, and with your cooperation for the Holy Spirit to work on your heart for it to be in the right condition for the anointing of the Holy Spirit empowerment. Heart transformation from desperately wicked stony state to a heart of flesh and love is a process and therefore takes time.

## Can God trust you with the anointing?

One of the reasons why God will not anoint a person is if that person cannot be trusted with the anointing of the Holy Spirit. God will train you, test you again and again till He is satisfied that you can be trusted with the anointing before He will finally anoint you.

If you give a child a gun, he can misuse it by shooting people and even himself because he was not properly trained and tested before he got the gun.

Similarly, God will only anoint people He has trained and tested very well. Those who have successfully been through the process will be anointed and empowered by the Holy Spirit. Can God trust you with the anointing, power, money, information etc? Can God trust you that you will not merchandise the anointing? That you will not charge money before you minister to people with God's anointing upon your life. That you will not charge people money before you give them a prophetic word. God will only anoint you when He can finally trust you. Note that if a person cannot be trusted, abundant anointing, power, blessings, and prosperity will not be given to the person. Be loyal and trustworthy both to men and God.

When God finally anoints you with Holy Ghost power, you will be deeply connected, and ***aligned*** with the Godhead, as you operate in the supernatural realm. Your life and ministry will be full of miracles, excellent results, and testimonies in Jesus' name. Amen!

## Touch not the anointed children of God

When God finally anoints you with Holy Ghost empowerment, you are promoted to become one of His untouchables. You have paid the price to successfully go through the crushing training and tests of the Most High God. You are now God's anointed. The Bible says in:

## Psalms 105:14-15

*14 He suffered no man to do them wrong: yea, he reproved kings for their sakes;*
*15 Saying, Touch not mine anointed, and do my prophets no harm.*

## Zechariah 2:8

*8 For thus saith the LORD of hosts; After the glory hath he sent me unto the nations which spoiled you: for he that toucheth you toucheth the apple of his eye.*

God has invested much time, and resources training you. So you are precious to Him, and He ensures that He guides, protects, preserves, and shields you from the attacks of wicked men, and satanic attacks as you faithfully accomplish the purpose and assignment for which He anointed you. Anyone who touches you with evil intentions is doing that to their own detriment. It will be instant judgement and punishment. God is a jealous God, and He fights for His anointed in a brutal manner that destroys enemies.

## Exodus 14:14

*14 The LORD shall fight for you, and ye shall hold your peace.*

**King David** – For example, God's anointed king David did not have to fight Nabal in 1 Samuel 25:38-39 for being rude and wicked to him. God smote Nabal.

**Abraham** – In James 2:23, and 2 Chronicles 20:7, Abraham was referred to as a "Friend of God" God said this about Abraham in:

## Genesis 12:3

*³ And I will bless them that bless thee, and curse him that curseth thee: and in thee shall all families of the earth be blessed.*

Will you dare curse a friend of God? No way! If you try it, it may even turn to generational curse. Therefore, hold your peace.

Do you mess about with a friend of God's wife? No way! Even if you are a king, He will reprove you. King Abimelech took Abraham's wife Sarah. Read what God said to him in:

## Genesis 20:2-3

*² And Abraham said of Sarah his wife, She is my sister: and Abimelech king of Gerar sent, and took Sarah.*

*³ But God came to Abimelech in a dream by night, and said to him, Behold, thou art but a dead man, for the woman which thou hast taken; for she is a man's wife.*

Can you see from the above scripture that you don't try nonsense with anointed Men and Women of God even if you are a king? God said, "*...Behold, thou art but a dead man...*" if you touch Sarah, Abraham's wife.

As God's anointed, you will enjoy many benefits, but ensure you don't misuse or abuse such benefits.

**King David** – The Bible tells us in *Psalm 89:20* that God anointed David with His holy oil. *Acts 13:22* also states that God said, "*...I have found David the son of Jesse, a man after mine own heart, which shall fulfil all my will.*

Note that when King David committed adultery with Bathsheba, Uriah's wife, and plotted for Uriah to be killed, God was furious, and ensured that he was punished. The child Bathsheba had for him died. You don't mess about with God or His people because you are anointed. You must behave yourself, or else God will deal with you.

***King Saul*** – After king Saul was anointed and ordained to be king, God instructed him to destroy all the Amalekites in 1 Samuel 15:3, but he did not fully obey the instruction, and that led to his dethronement as the king of Israel.

This should serve as a caution and warning for all God's anointed to be loving, obedient, and keep walking uprightly as a person of integrity. Be careful! If God did not spare King David, the man after God's own heart, then, who are you to be spared except for His mercy?

## CONCLUSION

*2 Corinthians 13:5*

<u>*Examine yourselves, whether ye be in the faith; prove your own selves*</u>. *Know ye not your own selves, how that Jesus Christ is in you, except ye be reprobates?* (Underline mine)

Now that you have read this chapter, I would like to suggest you do what the above scripture says. "*Examine yourselves, whether ye be in the faith; prove your own selves.*" Take a moment of time and reflect on your Christian walk so far by examining and testing yourself if you are truly in the faith. Based on your genuine assessment, draw up a plan you will follow to intentionally move up in your Christianity ladder. The path of the just is like the shining light that shines more and more unto the perfect day.

## NOTE

*Please note that the process of being anointed with Holy Ghost empowerment will not be exactly the same for everyone, but there would be some similarities based on biblical standards.*

*The process varies because we are all unique with different visions and dreams, under different situations and circumstances. God also passes us through different training and tests as He prepares us for different assignments and purposes. Therefore, I have given a general description of the process in this chapter. If there is anything I have stated that does not apply to you, simply put it aside, and hold on to the ones that apply to you. God bless you in Jesus' name. Amen!*

# CHAPTER TEN

# THE NINE GIFTS OF THE HOLY SPIRIT

*1 Corinthians 12:1-11*

*¹ Now concerning spiritual gifts, brethren, I would not have you ignorant.*

*² Ye know that ye were Gentiles, carried away unto these dumb idols, even as ye were led.*

*³ Wherefore I give you to understand, that no man speaking by the Spirit of God calleth Jesus accursed: and that no man can say that Jesus is the Lord, but by the Holy Ghost.*

*⁴ Now there are diversities of gifts, but the same Spirit.*

*⁵ And there are differences of administrations, but the same Lord.*

*⁶ And there are diversities of operations, but it is the same God which worketh all in all.*

*⁷ But the manifestation of the Spirit is given to every man to profit withal.*

*⁸ For to one is given by the Spirit the <u>word of wisdom</u>; to another the <u>word of knowledge</u> by the same Spirit;*

*⁹ To another <u>faith</u> by the same Spirit; to another the <u>gifts of healing</u> by the same Spirit;*

¹⁰ *To another the <u>working of miracles</u>; to another <u>prophecy</u>; to another <u>discerning of spirits</u>; to another <u>divers kinds of tongues</u>; to another the <u>interpretation of tongues</u>:*

¹¹ *But all these worketh that one and the selfsame Spirit, dividing to every man severally as he will.* (Underline mine)

The above passage of the Bible highlights the 9 gifts of the Holy Spirit. Verses 4-6, makes it clear that there are diversities of gifts but the same Spirit, differences in administrations, but the same Lord, diversities of operations, but the same Lord.

Verse 7, tells us that the gift is given to every man to profit withal. This means that the gift of the Holy Spirit given to a man is not for himself, but to serve others.

Verse 11, further makes it clear that the gifts are distributed by the Holy Spirit to believers in the church and body of Christ as He will. This means that the Holy Spirit decides who, when, how, where the gifts are used. No one has control over these gifts, but the Holy Spirit. All the gifts are operated by the inspiration of the Holy Spirit.

For clarity purposes, these gifts will be discussed below under three headings based on the functions of the gifts. Utterance or vocal gifts say something. The revelation gifts see and hear things. The power gifts are characterized by power to do things in their operation. These gifts are for the church, and the body of Christ, and should also benefit the individual. They all operate by the inspiration of the Holy Spirit.

### *Utterance gifts*

- Divers kinds of tongues
- Interpretation of tongues
- The gift of prophecy

## Revelation gifts

- Word of knowledge
- Word of wisdom
- Discerning of spirits

## Power gifts

- Gift of faith
- The gift of healing
- The working of miracles

## Utterance gifts

### Divers kinds of tongues

We have already discussed speaking in tongues as it relates to an individual in Chapter eight. However, our discussion here will focus on speaking in tongues in the church or other public gatherings. The Bible says in:

### 1 Corinthians 14:26-29

$^{26}$ *How is it then, brethren? when ye come together, <u>every one of you hath</u> a psalm, hath a doctrine, hath <u>a tongue</u>, hath a revelation, hath an interpretation. Let all things be done unto edifying.*

$^{27}$ <u>*If any man speak in an unknown tongue, let it be by two, or at the most by three*</u>*, and that by course; and <u>let one interpret</u>.*

$^{28}$ <u>*But if there be no interpreter, let him keep silence in the church; and let him speak to himself, and to God*</u>*.*

$^{29}$ *Let the prophets speak two or three, and let the other judge.* (Underline mine)

Apostle Paul gave us in the above scriptures a guideline on how we are to speak in tongues in the church and other public gatherings because all things must be done decently and in order. He says as we gather in church, let two or maximum of three people speak in tongues, while a person interprets. If there is no interpreter, he says we should keep silent and speak to ourselves and to God.

There can sometimes be counterfeit tongues. It's therefore important to pay attention, listen carefully as tongues are spoken in order to discern what is said, and pick out the voice of the enemy to deceive.

## Interpretation of tongues

Apostle Paul says in the scripture below that he that speaketh with tongues should pray that he may interpret. It's to your advantage that you are able to interpret your tongues and the tongues of others. This enables you to know the meaning of what is said, and exactly what to do next.

## 1 Corinthians 14:13

*Wherefore let him that speaketh in an unknown tongue pray that he may interpret.*

## 1 Corinthians 14:19

*Yet in the church I had rather speak five words with my understanding, that by my voice I might teach others also, than ten thousand words in an unknown tongue.*

Clarity in preaching the gospel is so important that the Apostle Paul had to say in the above scripture that he would rather speak five words for people to understand than ten thousand words with tongues that people may not understand.

Note that once tongues are interpreted, it brings it at par with prophecy. See 1 Corinthians 14:5. Again, interpretation of tongues is not done in the manner of translation like an earthly language. Tongue is a supernatural language, therefore the interpretation is also done with supernatural ability and manner. Interpretation of tongues is the least of all the 9 gifts of the Spirit because it is the only gift that depends on another gift (tongues) to function. No tongues, no interpretation!

## *The gift of prophecy*

The gift of prophecy is supernatural revelation of the mind of God through the inspiration of the Holy Spirit of something that will happen in the future. It is important to know that there is a difference between a prophetic inspired word you receive from the office of a prophet, and a word spoken to encourage you. Let's look at a few scriptures to distinguish these two.

### *Corinthians 14:3*

*But he that prophesieth speaketh unto men to edification, and exhortation, and comfort.*

The above scripture is talking about a word of encouragement to edify another, and not necessarily a prophetic word because it may not be inspired by the Holy Spirit, or given by a person holding the office of a Prophet.

### *Acts 21:8-11*

*⁸ And the next day we that were of Paul's company departed, and came unto Caesarea: and we entered into the house of <u>Philip the evangelist</u>, which was one of the seven; and abode with him.*

*⁹ And the same man <u>had four daughters, virgins, which did prophesy</u>.*

*¹⁰ And as we tarried there many days, there came down from Judaea a certain <u>prophet, named Agabus.</u>*

*¹¹ And when he was come unto us, <u>he took Paul's girdle</u>, and bound his own hands and feet, and said, <u>Thus saith the Holy Ghost,</u> So shall the Jews at Jerusalem bind the man that owneth this girdle, and shall deliver him into the hands of the Gentiles.* (Underline mine)

The above biblical passage beautifully gives us a difference between prophesying and prophetic words given by a prophet.

Evangelist Philip had four daughters who did prophesy. Was this prophesying inspired by the Holy Spirit? No! Did it make them prophetesses? No! Their prophesying was to edify, exhort, and comfort people which is great. We also see in the above passage a prophet of God, come with an inspired prophetic word. He took up Paul's girdle and said, "...*Thus saith the Holy Ghost,...*" What he said was inspired by the Holy Ghost. That's a prophetic word from the Holy Ghost regarding the future.

## Acts 11:28

And there stood up one of them named <u>Agabus</u>, and signified <u>by the Spirit</u> that there should be great <u>dearth</u> throughout all the world: <u>which came to pass</u> in the days of Claudius Caesar.

We see Prophet Agabus prophesy again by the Spirit that there will be famine. Again, this prophetic word was inspired by the Holy Spirit and it came to pass.

## How do you know a genuine prophetic word?

*First*, the prophetic word should come as a confirmation to what you already know or agree with.

*Second*, if the word of the prophet comes to pass or happens, then it is genuine. The Bible says in:

## Deuteronomy 18:22

*²² When a prophet speaketh in the name of the LORD, if the thing follow not, nor come to pass, that is the thing which the LORD hath not spoken, but the prophet hath spoken it presumptuously: thou shalt not be afraid of him.*

### Revelation gifts

### Word of knowledge

This is a supernatural word inspired by the Holy Spirit, and it usually relates to the *past or present*. This knowledge is not natural or academic knowledge. Note that this Word of knowledge is not the same as the Hosea 4:6 knowledge.

## John 4:18

*For thou hast had five husbands; and he whom thou now hast is not thy husband: in that saidst thou truly.*

Jesus asked the Samaritan woman by the well, to go and call her husband, but she said she doesn't have a husband. Then Jesus gave her a spot on word of knowledge about her five *past* marriages, and the present man she's with is not her husband. She marveled.

## 2 Kings 5:25-27

*²⁵ But he went in, and stood before his master. And Elisha said unto him, Whence comest thou, Gehazi? And he said, Thy servant went no whither.*

*²⁶ And he said unto him, Went not mine heart with thee, when the man turned again from his chariot to meet thee? Is it a time to receive money, and to receive garments, and oliveyards, and vineyards, and sheep, and oxen, and menservants, and maidservants?*

*²⁷ The leprosy therefore of Naaman shall cleave unto thee, and unto thy seed for ever. And he went out from his presence a leper as white as snow.*

The above Bible passage is another classic example demonstrating the word of knowledge about *present* situation in action. Prophet Elisha asked Gehazi where he went, and he said he went nowhere. And Prophet Elisha said to him, *"...Went not mine heart with thee..."* This statement confirms that there was a heart or spirit interaction between Elisha and Gehazi and Elisha saw in the realm of the spirit, and knew supernaturally what Gehazi did at that *present* time. This is not mind reading or clairvoyance. The Bible says in:

## 1 Corinthians 2:11

*For what man knoweth the things of a man, save the spirit of man which is in him? even so the things of God knoweth no man, but the Spirit of God.*

When you are in the Spirit, full of the Word of God which is the sword of the Spirit, you can pick up and discern the thoughts and intents of others just like Elisha knew the thoughts and actions of Gehazi. (See Hebrews 4:12).

## Word of wisdom

This is a supernatural word inspired by the Holy Spirit, and it usually relates to the *present* or the *future*. This wisdom is not natural as in having the ability to correctly apply knowledge. Note that this word of wisdom is not the same as the James 1:5 wisdom.

## Acts 9:10-16

*¹⁰ And there was a certain disciple at Damascus, named <u>Ananias</u>; and to him said the Lord in a <u>vision</u>, Ananias. And he said, Behold, I am here, Lord.*

*¹¹ <u>And the Lord said unto him, Arise, and go into the street which is called Straight, and enquire in the house of Judas for one called Saul, of Tarsus: for, behold, he prayeth,</u>*

*¹² And hath seen in a vision a man named Ananias coming in, and putting his hand on him, that he might receive his sight.*

¹³ Then Ananias answered, Lord, I have heard by many of this man, how much evil he hath done to thy saints at Jerusalem:

¹⁴ And here he hath authority from the chief priests to bind all that call on thy name.

*¹⁵ But the Lord said unto him, Go thy way: for he is a chosen vessel unto me, to bear my name before the Gentiles, and kings, and the children of Israel:*

*¹⁶ For I will shew him how great things he must suffer for my name's sake.* (Underline mine)

The above biblical passage is an interplay between word of knowledge and word of wisdom in operation. The words are given simultaneously. Let's examine it further.

Verse 10 tells us that the disciple named Ananias was in a vision. And in verse 11, he got a word from Lord Jesus telling him to go and minister to Saul, and gave him the address, and said that he will find him praying. This is a word of knowledge because it is for the *present*.

We also see from verse 12 above that at that same time, Saul also saw a vision that Ananias was coming to him to put his hand on him to receive his sight. This is also feedback for the *present*.

In verse 15-16, we see our Lord Jesus declaring to Ananias that Saul is a chosen vessel unto him to preach the gospel, and He will show him the great things he must suffer for His name's sake. This statement is a word of wisdom because it relates to the *future*.

It's important to note that visions and dreams can sometimes be a vehicle of transportation of word of knowledge and word of wisdom as we have seen above with visions. Before Joseph became the Prime Minister of Egypt, God revealed it to him in a dream in

Genesis 37. Before famine struck Egypt, God revealed it in a dream to the pharaoh, and Joseph interpreted the dream in Genesis 41.

## Discerning of spirits

This supernatural gift of discerning of spirits is the ability to hear, and see into the realm of the spirit with precision to know what's happening through the inspiration of the Holy Spirit. This is also equivalent to supernaturally perceiving things accurately through the inspiration of the Holy Spirit.

## 2 Kings 6:15-17

*15 And when the <u>servant of the man of God</u> was risen early, and gone forth, behold, an <u>host compassed the city both with horses and chariots.</u> And his servant said unto him, <u>Alas, my master! how shall we do</u>?*

*16 And he answered, Fear not: for they that be with us are more than they that be with them.*

*17 <u>And Elisha prayed, and said, LORD, I pray thee, open his eyes, that he may see. And the LORD opened the eyes of the young man; and he saw:</u> and, behold, the mountain was full of horses and chariots of fire round about Elisha.* (Underline mine)

Note from the above biblical passage that Prophet Elisha's servant was afraid that they were compassed by horses and chariots and cried out to his master Elisha. And Elisha said to him in verse 16... *"Fear not: for they that be with us are more than they that be with them..."* However, his servant could not see what Elisha was seeing because you cannot see into the spirit realm with your physical natural eyes. No! You can only see into the spirit realm with your spiritual eyes. That's why you have to be in the Spirit to be able to operate in the spirit realm. You can't access the spirit realm in the flesh.

In verse 17, Elisha prayed to the LORD to open his servant's eyes to see, and the LORD opened his eyes and he saw the mountain was full of horses and chariots to help them. Was he blind before? No! This is a confirmation that you need to evolve, and be in the Spirit in order to interact with spirits in the supernatural realm.

## 1 Kings 22:19

*And he said, Hear thou therefore the word of the LORD: I saw the LORD sitting on his throne, and all the host of heaven standing by him on his right hand and on his left.*

King Ahab and Jehoshaphat consulted 400 prophets who told them that they will go to battle and win and take over Ramothgilead. However, Prophet Micaiah saw the LORD in the Spirit in the above scripture and interacted with the spirit realm before he spoke on the contrary and King Ahab wasn't happy. The LORD sent lying spirits into the 400 prophets, and Ahab died in the battle. You can see that the spirit realm is superior to the natural realm, and to be in the Spirit is superior to be in the flesh.

## Acts 7:55-56

*⁵⁵ But he, being full of the Holy Ghost, looked up stedfastly into heaven, and saw the glory of God, and Jesus standing on the right hand of God,*

*⁵⁶ And said, Behold, I see the heavens opened, and the Son of man standing on the right hand of God.*

The above is the account of Stephen. The scripture tells us that he was full of the Holy Ghost, looked into heaven, and saw the glory of God, and Jesus on the right hand of God. This is Stephen seeing into the realm of the spirit shortly before he died.

## Power gifts

### Gift of faith

The gift of faith is a supernatural impartation of faith by the Holy Spirit upon a person to perform a special task in an instant as that window of opportunity is opened at that moment. Once that moment is gone, that Spirit of faith expires. It is not something that can be accomplished by applying a principle or formula to produce a repeated result. The Holy Spirit inspires this gift of faith and therefore He is in control of who, when, how, and where it operates. Note that this gift of faith is not the same as the Hebrews 11:1, Romans 10:17, and Ephesians 2:8 faith.

### Samson

### Judges 15:14-15

*¹⁴ And when he came unto Lehi, the Philistines shouted against him: and <u>the Spirit of the LORD came mightily upon him</u>, and the cords that were upon his arms became as flax that was burnt with fire, and his bands loosed from off his hands.*

*¹⁵ And he found a new <u>jawbone of an ass</u>, and put forth his hand, and took it, and <u>slew a thousand men therewith</u>.* (Underline mine)

Samson slew a thousand men with the jawbone of an ass. This is a supernatural action performed by Samson in that moment because the Spirit of the Lord came upon him mightily and he acted by the gift of faith in operation at that particular time. Now if Samson tried to do a repeat of this same act, at any other time, he may not even kill anyone with the same jawbone because the gift of faith aided by the Spirit of God upon him at this time is not in operation.

### The gift of healing

The gift of healing is also a supernatural impartation of healing by the Holy Spirit upon a person to perform a special healing task in an instant as that window of opportunity is opened at that moment. Once that moment is gone, that Spirit of healing expires. It is not something that can be accomplished by applying a principle or formula to produce a repeated result. The Holy Spirit inspires this gift of healing and therefore is in control of who, when, how, and where it operates.

## Acts 14:8-10

⁸ *And there sat <u>a certain man at Lystra</u>, impotent in his feet, being a <u>cripple</u> from his mother's womb, who never had walked:*

⁹ *The same heard <u>Paul speak</u>: who stedfastly beholding him, and <u>perceiving</u> that he <u>had faith to be healed</u>,*

¹⁰ *Said with a loud voice, Stand upright on thy feet. <u>And he leaped and walked</u>.* (Underline mine)

The above is a scenario showing an interplay between the gift of healing and faith in operation. Paul perceived that the cripple had faith to be healed at that particular moment, and straightaway ministered to the man and he was healed instantly. Now if Paul had tried a repeat of that same healing at another time, it may not happen.

It's important to note that there are some people specially gifted in the area of healing and therefore known as healing ministers because they are known to manifest this gift regularly with outstanding results. With this sort of person, healing happens a lot in their ministry because they hold that office of healing gift.

## The working of miracles

A miracle is an extraordinary, exceptional, supernatural event that happens which cannot be explained by natural or scientific laws, and therefore attributed to a divine agency. When an event is termed to be a miracle, then it is of God and nothing else. Let's look at some biblical examples.

**Moses** – *red sea parted with a rod*

## Exodus 14:21

*And Moses stretched out his hand over the sea; and the LORD caused the sea to go back by a strong east wind all that night, and made the sea dry land, and the waters were divided.*

Moses performed many miracles and the above is one of them. The red sea was parted when the Egyptians gave them a hot chase, and the Israelites crossed on dry land. Miracle! In another scenario which we saw earlier in Chapter five, his rod swallowed up the rods of Pharaoh's magicians that became serpents in Exodus 7. And in another account, he spoke and the earth opened up and swallowed Korah, Dathan, Abiram, and their families in Numbers 16. This is a man demonstrating the gift of miracles.

**Peter** – preached powerfully and people received salvation and his shadow healed people. It's important to note that it is the Holy Spirit that inspires these miracles working in and through men.

## Acts 5:14-16

[14] *And believers were the more added to the Lord, multitudes both of men and women.)*

[15] *Insomuch that they brought forth the sick into the streets, and laid them on beds and couches, that at the least the shadow of Peter passing by might overshadow some of them.*

[16] *There came also a multitude out of the cities round about unto Jerusalem, bringing sick folks, and them which were vexed with unclean spirits: and they were healed every one.*

## Gifts for supporting the Saints of God

Apart from the 9 gifts of the Holy Spirit which we just discussed above, we also have other gifts recorded in the Word of God. While the 9 gifts are Holy Spirit inspired and administered, these gifts are sort of distributed among believers as talents to be recognised and developed.

*Romans 12:6-8*

*⁶ Having then gifts differing according to the grace that is given to us, whether prophecy, let us prophesy according to the proportion of faith;*

*⁷ Or ministry, let us wait on our ministering: or he that teacheth, on teaching;*

*⁸ Or he that exhorteth, on exhortation: he that giveth, let him do it with simplicity; he that ruleth, with diligence; he that sheweth mercy, with cheerfulness.*

- Prophesying – Encouraging and edifying the saints of God
- Ministering – Choir, hospitality, evangelism, media, finance, security etc.
- Teaching – Sunday school teacher, Youth leader, support worker
- Exhortation – Encouraging the saints of God
- Giving – Supporting church projects financially, giving alms and donations
- Ruler – Supporting the church with your administrative and leadership skills
- Mercy – Be a person to support people in trouble by being lenient

Note that as a born again Christian, you have to search within you and recognise at least one or more of the above gifts that you will start operating in to support believers, the church, and the body of Christ. God created everyone with at least one of the above gifts. No excuses! Be relevant in the vineyard of the Lord.

## The fivefold ministry

These are offices assigned to different people in the body of Christ to help with proper administration and organisation of the church, perfecting the saints, the work of the ministry, and the body of Christ.

*Ephesians 4:11-12*

*[11] And he gave some, apostles; and some, prophets; and some, evangelists; and some, pastors and teachers;*

*[12] For the perfecting of the saints, for the work of the ministry, for the edifying of the body of Christ:*

## Qualifications of a Bishop

These are the qualifications anyone who desires to be a Bishop should have. However, to some extent, it also applies to the entire 5 fold ministry offices.

*1 Timothy 3:1-7*

*[1] This is a true saying, If a man desire the office of a bishop, he desireth a good work.*

*[2] A bishop then must be blameless, the husband of one wife, vigilant, sober, of good behaviour, given to hospitality, apt to teach;*

*[3] Not given to wine, no striker, not greedy of filthy lucre; but patient, not a brawler, not covetous;*

*[4] One that ruleth well his own house, having his children in subjection with all gravity;*

*[5] (For if a man know not how to rule his own house, how shall he take care of the church of God?)*

⁶ *Not a novice, lest being lifted up with pride he fall into the condemnation of the devil.*

⁷ *Moreover he must have a good report of them which are without; lest he fall into reproach and the snare of the devil.*

## Ephesians 4:11-12

¹¹ *And he gave some, apostles; and some, prophets; and some, evangelists; and some, pastors and teachers;*

¹² *For the perfecting of the saints, for the work of the ministry, for the edifying of the body of Christ:*

## Apostles

Apostle in Greek means, *a sent one, messenger, or commissioned one.* The office of an Apostle involves teaching the gospel, establishing doctrines and churches, missionary trips, and uniting the saints in the body of Christ.

Jesus is our first Apostle as the scripture below states.

## Hebrews 3:1

*Wherefore, holy brethren, partakers of the heavenly calling, consider the Apostle and High Priest of our profession, Christ Jesus;*

The scripture below also states that Jesus is the Shepherd and Bishop of our souls.

## 1 Peter 2:25

*For ye were as sheep going astray; but are now returned unto the Shepherd and Bishop of your souls.*

The second set of Apostles are the 12 Apostles that walked directly with our Lord Jesus. See Luke 6:12-16, and Mark 3:16-19 for a list of them.

The next set of Apostles is only Apostle Paul who though did not walk directly with Jesus Christ, was specially called and anointed by the Lord. That's why he had so many revelations and authored about two third of the New Testament epistles, established biblical doctrines, planted many churches, embarked on many missionary trips, taught and preached the gospel.

The fourth level Apostles are present day Apostles. They are also to operate in line with the qualifications given earlier. When you are called to be an Apostle, or any of the other fivefold ministry, there are certain things that will happen. For example, you will experience an encounter, and He will clearly spell out your calling to a geographical area, or to a people. He will also give you your mandate with specific strategies. Jesus was called to the lost sheep of the house of Israel – See Matthew 15:24. Jesus spelt out the geographical area of jurisdiction for the 12 Apostles in Matthew 10:5-6. They are to go to the lost sheep of the house of Israel. Apostle Paul was sent to the uncircumcision – See Galatians 2:7. As good as preaching the gospel is, he was stopped from preaching in Asia in Acts 16:6-7. He also had an encounter with Jesus, asked Him for his mandate – See Acts 9:6, and 1 Corinthians 9:1. Where and who are you called to as an Apostle? Read what the Bible says below about false Apostles.

## *2 Corinthians 11:13*

*For such are false apostles, deceitful workers, transforming themselves into the apostles of Christ.*

The above scripture brings to our awareness that there are false apostles transforming themselves into apostles of Christ. How can you detect a false apostle? If they are acting contrary to the outlined qualifications above. Besides, you have to test all spirits.

## *Prophets*

The office of a prophet in the Old Testament usually has to do with foretelling *future* events as God's spokesperson.

That's why we see in the Bible great prophets of God like Isaiah, Elijah, Elisha, Jeremiah, Ezekiel etc. saying, *"Thus saith the Lord…"*

## Some things to note about prophets and prophecies

*A true prophetic word from God declared by a prophet will happen*

### Deuteronomy 18:22

*22 When a prophet speaketh in the name of the LORD, if the thing follow not, nor come to pass, that is the thing which the LORD hath not spoken, but the prophet hath spoken it presumptuously: thou shalt not be afraid of him.*

The above scripture states that when a prophet of God speaks and it does not come to pass, then what he said is not of God.

### Negative prophetic word can be reversed

Note that a negative prophetic word can be reversed. If your spirit does not accept a negative prophecy, then you should reject it. The prophet should as a matter of fact also pray and bind negative prophecies from manifesting as they are being revealed. Prophecies should be for edification, exhortation, and comfort. The Bible says in:

### Isaiah 38:1-5

*1 In those days was Hezekiah sick unto death. And Isaiah the prophet the son of Amoz came unto him, and said unto him, Thus saith the LORD, Set thine house in order: for thou shalt die, and not live.*

*2 Then Hezekiah turned his face toward the wall, and prayed unto the LORD,*

*³ And said, Remember now, O LORD, I beseech thee, how I have walked before thee in truth and with a perfect heart, and have done that which is good in thy sight. And Hezekiah wept sore.*

*⁴ Then came the word of the LORD to Isaiah, saying,*

*⁵ Go, and say to Hezekiah, Thus saith the LORD, the God of David thy father, I have heard thy prayer, I have seen thy tears: behold, I will add unto thy days fifteen years.*

In the above scriptures we see King Hezekiah reversing in prayer the sad news by Prophet Isaiah that he will die. Well, King Hezekiah is not yet ready to die, so he prayed to God reminding Him of how he has walked with Him in truth and with a perfect heart. And God reversed the death sentence by adding another 15 years to him. It's interesting to note that God did not dispute the grounds the king asked Him to consider again. God agreed that the king was indeed a man of integrity. This means that as Christians we also have to walk before God in truth and with a perfect heart so that when we also come boldly before His throne He will grant our petitions. Hallelujah!

*Believe in your prophet of God and prosper*

## 2 Chronicles 20:20

*And they rose early in the morning, and went forth into the wilderness of Tekoa: and as they went forth, Jehoshaphat stood and said, Hear me, O Judah, and ye inhabitants of Jerusalem; Believe in the LORD your God, so shall ye be established; <u>believe his prophets, so shall ye prosper</u>.* (Underline mine)

Do you want to prosper? Believe in your prophet of God and you will prosper as stated in the above scripture.

*Before God will do a thing, he will reveal it to a trusted prophet*

The Bible says in:

## Amos 3:7

*Surely the Lord GOD will do nothing, but he revealeth his secret unto his servants the prophets.*

## 2 Kings 4:27

*And when she came to the man of God to the hill, she caught him by the feet: but Gehazi came near to thrust her away. And the man of God said, Let her alone; <u>for her soul is vexed within her: and the LORD hath hid it from me, and hath not told me.</u>* (Underline mine)

The underlined scripture is a scenario between Prophet Elisha and the Shunammite woman. She lost her son and was vexed within her. And Prophet Elisha said, the LORD hid it from me and did not tell me. This means that God may not tell a prophet everything. Is this a contradiction to Amos 3:7? No! God is sovereign, and has the veto power to reveal what He considers should be revealed. Perhaps this is one He does not consider should be revealed.

*There are many false prophets in the world*

## 1 John 4:1

*Beloved, believe not every spirit, but try the spirits whether they are of God: because many false prophets are gone out into the world.*

The above scripture is warning believers to beware because there are many false prophets in the world. The scripture goes on to say we have to try the spirits whether they are of God. How do you try the spirits? By judging what a prophet says with the Word of God. Does my spirit agree with what he says? Apply wisdom and depend on the Holy Spirit to lead you. If it fails the Word of God test, you may need to trash it.

## Don't despise prophecies

*1 Thessalonians 5:20 - Despise not prophesyings.* Note that the fact that there are many false prophets in the world should not make you despise prophecies. No! Still have an open mind approach to prophecies until you test and prove them right or wrong.

In the New Testament, the office of a prophet is also very relevant because they are here to help in pioneering a church, preaching and teaching the gospel, and helping to unite believers in the body of Christ.

## Evangelists

Evangelists are also servants of God in the fivefold ministry. Evangelists engage in revivals, and crusades where signs, wonders, miracles, salvation, deliverances, and healings happen. They teach and preach the gospel, lead people to Christ, and help to unite the church and the body of Christ. They are missionaries on the move because they move about preaching the gospel. Philip the Evangelist exemplifies the ministry of an evangelist. The Bible says in:

### Acts 8:5-8

*⁵ Then Philip went down to the city of Samaria, and preached Christ unto them.*

*⁶ And the people with one accord gave heed unto those things which Philip spake, hearing and seeing the miracles which he did.*

*⁷ For unclean spirits, crying with loud voice, came out of many that were possessed with them: and many taken with palsies, and that were lame, were healed.*

*⁸ And there was great joy in that city.*

## Pastors

Pastors also hold an office in the fivefold ministry as called servants of God. Pastors are responsible to look after the flock God has committed to them. They are like shepherds leading flocks.

### Acts 20:28

*Take heed therefore unto yourselves, and to all the flock, over the which the Holy Ghost hath made you overseers, <u>to feed the church of God</u>, which he hath purchased with his own blood.* (Underline mine)

The above scripture makes it clear that a pastor has to feed the church of God. With what? The Word of God. That is the number one food a congregation needs. This means that a pastor should spend quality time in the Word of God to be able to draw out new revelations to share with the congregation. The Bible says again in:

### Jeremiah 3:15

*And I will give you pastors according to mine heart, which shall feed you with knowledge and understanding.*

You see again that God is saying in the above scripture that He will give us pastors according to His heart who will feed the congregation with knowledge and understanding. Therefore, a pastor must be prepared to teach and preach. To teach has to do with explaining the gospel, while preaching has to do with proclaiming the gospel.

## Teachers

Everyone called to the fivefold ministry should have the ability to teach. However, those called to the office of teachers specifically display special teaching skills and ability obviously because of the unique anointing to perform this task.

I would like to mention here that this call to be a teacher is not the same as a person attending a seminary school, Bible college, and college of Theology and claiming to be called by God as a teacher. No! The same applies to other offices of the fivefold ministry. Attending a seminary school, Bible College, or studying Theology is an added advantage to your call by God. Attending the schools and teaching the Word of God, without the call of God does not mean you are called by God. Read what the Word of God says below:

*Psalms 89:20*

*I have found David my servant; with my holy oil have I anointed him:*

*Acts 13:2*

*As they ministered to the Lord, and fasted, <u>the Holy Ghost said</u>, Separate me <u>Barnabas</u> and <u>Saul</u> for the <u>work</u> whereunto <u>I have called them</u>.* (Underline mine)

*Hebrews 5:4*

*And no man taketh this honour unto himself, but <u>he that is called of God, as was Aaron.</u>* (Underline mine)

It's better and more honourable to allow God to call a man into any of the fivefold ministry. As you can see in the above scriptures, David, Barnabas, Saul, and Aaron were called by God as men of God. But today we see men who either called themselves, or another man called them. By their fruits ye shall know them. When God calls you, He will back you up by giving you *training*, a *vision*, and also make *provisions* for your ministry.

## Some things to note about teachers and teachings

*Do what you teach*: One important word for teachers is that they are under obligation to do what they teach. If you don't do what you teach, that amounts to hypocrisy. This is how Jesus put it in:

### Matthew 23:1-3

*¹ Then spake Jesus to the multitude, and to his disciples,*

*² Saying, The scribes and the Pharisees sit in Moses' seat:*

*³ All therefore whatsoever they bid you observe, that observe and do; but do not ye after their works: for they say, and do not.*

Simply put, Jesus said to the multitude and His disciples in the above scriptures, observe and do what the Pharisees bid you but don't do what they do. Why? Because they say the right things, but do the wrong things. As a teacher, you must do what you teach otherwise you are a Pharisee. You have to be a good example of what you teach. Read what the Bible recorded about Ezra in:

### Ezra 7:10

*For <u>Ezra</u> had prepared his heart to <u>seek the law of the LORD</u>, and <u>to do it</u>, and <u>to teach</u> in Israel statutes and judgments.* (Underline mine)

Ezra was a great man of God. He sought the law of the Lord, practiced it, and taught it in Israel. That's what the above scripture tells us. And that's what is expected of a teacher, and the rest of the holders of the fivefold ministry offices. Practice what you teach.

### Romans 2:21

*Thou therefore which <u>teachest</u> another, <u>teachest thou not thyself?</u> <u>thou that preachest a man should not steal, dost thou steal</u>?* (Underline mine)

*Matthew 5:19*

*Whosoever therefore shall <u>break</u> one of these least <u>commandments</u>, and shall <u>teach</u> men so, he shall be called the <u>least</u> in the kingdom of heaven: <u>but whosoever shall do and teach them</u>, the same shall be called <u>great</u> in the kingdom of heaven.* (Underline mine)

*Preach the word:*

*2 Timothy 4:2-4*

² *<u>Preach the word</u>; be instant in season, out of season; reprove, rebuke, exhort with all longsuffering and doctrine.*

³ *For the time will come when they will not endure sound doctrine; but after their own lusts shall they heap to themselves <u>teachers, having itching ears</u>;*

⁴ *<u>And they shall turn away their ears from the truth</u>, and shall be turned unto fables.* (Underline mine)

The above scripture from Apostle Paul to Pastor Timothy says, "Preach the Word." Teach the truth in the Word of God fearlessly, and without watering it down. Teach and preach as you are led by the Holy Spirit. Some people who have itchy ears will want you to teach what they want but ignore them.

## Further ministry offices and gifts

*1 Corinthians 12:28*

*And God hath set some in the church, first apostles, secondarily prophets, thirdly teachers, after that miracles, then gifts of healings, helps, governments, diversities of tongues.*

- Apostles – See above
- Prophets – See above
- Teachers – See above

- Miracles – Relates to evangelists
- Gifts of healings – Relates to evangelists
- Helps – Relates to choir, hospitality, media etc
- Governments – Relates to pastors and administrators
- Diversities of tongues – Relates to ministers

Apostle Paul made further lists of ministry offices and gifts as shown above. As you can see, we have already dealt with some of them in our earlier discussion.

# CHAPTER ELEVEN

# THE NINE FRUIT OF THE HOLY SPIRIT

When we receive salvation, Christ dwells in us, and the Holy Spirit interacts with our human spirit and the fruit of the Spirit is activated to start growing and with our cooperation it matures. The Holy Spirit works in us and through us to others. The fruit is singular not plural as in fruits. It is one *fruit* with nine parts embedded in it. The Bible says in:

*Galatians 5:22-23*

[22] But the <u>fruit</u> of the Spirit is love, joy, peace, longsuffering, gentleness, goodness, <u>faith,</u>

[23] Meekness, temperance: against such there is no law. (Underline mine)

*Galatians 5:22-23 New International Version (NIV)*

[22] But the fruit of the Spirit is love, joy, peace, forbearance, kindness, goodness, faithfulness,

[23] gentleness and self-control. Against such things there is no law.

*Galatians 5:22-23 New Living Translation (NLT)*

[22] But the Holy Spirit produces this kind of fruit in our lives: love, joy, peace, patience, kindness, goodness, faithfulness,

²³ *gentleness, and self-control. There is no law against these things!*

- Love
- Joy
- Peace
- Longsuffering, forbearance, patience
- Gentleness, kindness, kindness
- Goodness
- Faith, faithfulness, faithfulness
- Meekness, gentleness, gentleness
- Temperance, self-control, self-control

The above scriptures show the 9 fruit of the Spirit as recorded in Galatians 5:22-23 of the KJV, NIV, and NLT. I had to lay them side by side so that you can compare the above translations. Can you spot any difference?

As you can see from the KJV, I underlined *faith* because it does not appear to be right in KJV. The correct Greek translation is *faithfulness* as recorded in NIV and NLT above.

Again, you can also see that for example, longsuffering in KJV is translated as forbearance in NIV, and patience in NLT. However, they seem to be close synonyms and that's probably why they are used interchangeably.

It's important to note that unlike the gifts of the Holy Spirit distributed among believers, every saint of God should have all the fruit of the Holy Spirit.

The primary reason for the 9 fruit of the Holy Spirit in the life of a believer is to help him grow and mature with good character and habits to become Christ-like. The Bible says in: *Matthew 7:20, "Wherefore by their fruits ye shall know them."* The kind of fruit and lifestyle a Christian manifests is a reflection of what's going on inside them, and the extent of their growth, and maturity. Let's move on and examine each fruit further.

## Love

Love in Greek means *Agape*[11]. This is the unconditional love of Christ. Love is also known as charity. This love is the primary fruit of the 9 fruit of the Spirit. The Bible says in:

### Romans 5:5

*And hope maketh not ashamed; because the love of God is shed abroad in our hearts by the Holy Ghost which is given unto us.*

The Holy Spirit sheds the love of God in the hearts of born again Christians. This helps us to grow and mature. God is love, and because we are created in the image and likeness of God, we are to also love. As a matter of fact, Jesus commanded us to love one another in:

### John 13:34-35

[34] *A new commandment I give unto you, That ye love one another; as I have loved you, that ye also love one another.*

[35] *By this shall all men know that ye are my disciples, if ye have love one to another.*

By their fruits you shall know them. The love of God a believer displays shows their character and maturity in Christ. We have to intentionally yield and cooperate with the Holy Spirit to work in us and through us as the love of God is shed abroad in our hearts.

### Matthew 5:44

*But I say unto you, Love your enemies, bless them that curse you, do good to them that hate you, and pray for them which despitefully use you, and persecute you;*

The above scripture is a true test of mature love in a Christian. When you grow in love, you will mature to the point that you will love your enemies. You are able to forgive enemies easily. Read below what Jesus said about those who beat and crucified Him in:

## Luke 23:34

*Then said Jesus, Father, forgive them; for they know not what they do. And they parted his raiment, and cast lots.*

As believers, we have to love others. Love yourself, but don't become selfish. Love your family because charity begins at home. Love fellow Christians in the church, the body of Christ and others. Love everybody!

## Joy

Joy is an internal emotion inspired by the Holy Ghost, while happiness is external. Joy means *Chara*[12] in Greek. A believer must always jealously guard their joy because it is priceless. You lose joy, you've lost everything.

## Romans 14:17

*For the kingdom of God is not meat and drink; but righteousness, and peace, <u>and joy in the Holy Ghost</u>.* (Underline mine)

*Philippians 4:4 - Rejoice in the Lord alway: and again I say, Rejoice.*

## 1 Thessalonians 5:18

*In every thing give thanks: for this is the will of God in Christ Jesus concerning you.*

How can a person maintain a lifestyle of joy as a believer? By being in His presence. Psalm 16:11 says, "*...In your presence* *there is fullness of joy..."* also, by being thankful to God in everything. Don't ever complain. Always rejoice in the Lord. This is the day the Lord has made, rejoice and be glad in it. Dance and celebrate unto the Lord no matter the situation and circumstances. See Habakkuk 3:17-18. The joy of the Lord is our strength. See Nehemiah 8:10. When a person loses joy, they have lost strength. Preserve your strength by being joyful. Continually yield and cooperate with the Holy Spirit by being obedient, and He will impart more joy in you and through you as a Christian.

## *Peace*

Peace is the condition of quietness, and tranquility. Peace in Hebrew is *Salom*[13], and in Greek, it means *Eirene*[14]. A believer must always jealously guard their peace because it is priceless. Peace is a powerful tool of a Christian in the sense that God uses it as a means to lead us. When you are making enquiry from the Lord or facing a situation that requires direction or decision, absolute peace about that matter is an indication of green light or go ahead, but when you lose your peace about the matter it indicates red light, stop, danger, don't go ahead. A Christian must not ignore the prompting of peace from within as a signal.

As we grow in our Christian walk, we can deliberately cultivate and mature in peace. You have to deliberately make the decision to walk away from anything that will rob you of your peace. No peace could mean trouble, and that's unhealthy. No peace, no progress.

## *Hebrews 12:14*

*Follow peace with all men, and holiness, without which no man shall see the Lord:*

Some years ago, I did a study on the subject of peace. One of the things I discovered was that peace may sometimes not be cheap to achieve. You may have to pay a price sometimes to achieve peace as a Christian, if you don't apply the right wisdom. Thank God for the Holy Spirit, our Helper. The Author of Hebrews says in the above scripture, *"Follow peace with all men...."* Not some men, but *all* men. Does all men include murderers, robbers, liars, enemies etc? Now if you are right on a matter, and you still have to follow the offender with peace, you are paying a price to do so as a Christian, especially if you have to compromise on your values, and also humble yourself just to make peace. You say "Sorry" even if you are right. Let me explain further by telling you what King David said in:

*Psalms 34:14 - Depart from evil, and do good; seek peace, and pursue it.*

To seek peace and pursue it, can cost you your time, money, and other resources because you are negotiating and pleading with a person, or a people who don't agree with you. They believe they are right, and you are wrong. Can you see now that peace can sometimes come with a price? As I researched further I discovered this scripture below by Apostle Paul.

*Romans 12:18 - <u>If it be possible,</u> as much as lieth in you, live peaceably with all men.* (Underline mine)

When I read, *"If it be possible,..."* I said there seems to be a loophole here to escape from men who seem impossible. I thought, if I try to seek peace with those who seem impossible, and they don't agree, I will just leave them alone. But is that the right answer? Have you tried the Holy Spirit approach? The Holy Spirit approach always works. All you have to do is increase your communion with the Holy Spirit. And He will impart you with more grace, peace, and joy as you fellowship with Him. I will give you three scriptures below to express what will happen as you commune with the Holy Spirit.

*Exodus 14:14 - The LORD shall fight for you, and ye shall hold your peace.*

*Proverbs 16:7 - When a man's ways please the LORD, he maketh even his enemies to be at peace with him.*

*Philippians 4:7 - And the peace of God, which passeth all understanding, shall keep your hearts and minds through Christ Jesus.*

We have to get into the realm of enjoying internal and external peace that passeth all understanding. Let the Holy Spirit work in you, and through you as a Christian.

## PRAYER FOR YOU

*2 Thessalonians 3:16*

*Now the Lord of peace himself give you peace always by all means. The Lord be with you all.* In Jesus' name. Amen!

### *Longsuffering*

Longsuffering, forbearance, or patience is the ability to wait for something while we still have the right attitude. While we are waiting, we must continue to do the right things cheerfully. I prefer the word patience. Impatience is a sign of being in a hurry, and that signifies immaturity. Let the Holy Spirit work on you to build you up as you wait on the Lord.

### *James 1:2-4*

*[2] My brethren, count it all joy when ye fall into divers temptations;*

*[3] Knowing this, that the trying of your faith worketh patience.*

*[4] But let patience have her perfect work, that ye may be perfect and entire, wanting nothing.*

As challenging and crushing as it may be, God uses the time of longsuffering to build us up. Our faith is also built up, and perfected. Babies cry out for their food and want to get it right now, but adults can wait longer for the food to be cooked. Crying out loud to God to bless you right now can sometimes be a sign of babyhood. We need to grow up. If God does not release the blessings to us now, that means He considers us unprepared, and immature for the blessing and He wants to avoid misuse, and abuse of what we desire. What would a 12 year old child asking for a car do with the car if you give it? Crash it! God will delay the blessing of the car until the child grows up and matures to be at least 18 years and have a driving license.

Don't disrupt the patience process by being impatient. *"But let patience have her perfect work, that ye may be perfect and entire, wanting nothing."*

Jesus waited 30 years before His ministry started

Moses waited 40 years before his ministry started at the age of 80 years

Abraham had Isaac at the age of 100 years

Isaac married Rebecca at the age of 40 and had Esau and Jacob at the age of 60 years. He waited for 20 years. See Genesis 25:20 & 26.

Be patient! God's time is always the best. He never comes too early or too late. His timing is always perfect. Good things in life take time to build.

## 1 Peter 5:10

*But the God of all grace, who hath called us unto his eternal glory by Christ Jesus, <u>after that ye have suffered a while</u>, make you perfect, stablish, strengthen, settle you.* (Underline mine)

The problem with some people is that they don't want to do what the above scripture says. It says, "*...after that ye have suffered a* *while,…"* God will make you perfect, establish, strengthen, and settle you. It has to be pressure before pleasure, and not pleasure before pressure. Be patient! Can you see why KJV called it longsuffering, instead of short suffering?

## *Ecclesiastes 7:8*

*Better is the end of a thing than the beginning thereof: <u>and the patient in spirit is better than the proud in spirit.</u>* (Underline mine)

## **Gentleness**

Gentleness or kindness is the quality of being tender, and mild in character. The Holy Spirit works in us to impart this as we yield. The Bible says in:

## *Ephesians 4:32*

*And be ye kind one to another, tenderhearted, forgiving one another, even as God for Christ's sake hath forgiven you.*

Be kind to others. Consider helping strangers, orphans, widows, elderly, disabled, and other vulnerable people in the society. Support them with alms and donations, give out those items you have at home which you don't use again but are still in very good condition like your clothes, shoes, hand bags, plates, cups, cutlery, and other kitchen and household items. That's the true nature of a Christian displaying the character of Christ. Jesus walked on earth showing love, compassion, and kindness. Note that God will also reward you for these acts of kindness, and open doors of favor and blessings for you. *Acts 20:35* says, *"…It is more blessed to give than to receive."* Be a giver!

## **Goodness**

This has to do with upholding a moral virtuous character as a Christian. The Bible says in:

*Psalms 33:5*

*He loveth righteousness and judgment:*
*the earth is full of the goodness of the LORD.* Enjoy it!

## PRAYER FOR YOU

*Psalms 23:6*

*Surely goodness and mercy shall follow me all the days of my life: and I will dwell in the house of the LORD for ever.* In Jesus' name. Amen!

### *Faithfulness*

As I mentioned earlier, faithfulness as in the quality of being *loyal* is the correct translation and not faith as stated in Hebrews 11:1 or Romans 10:17. The Holy Spirit imparts a believer with the grace to be faithful. Faithfulness is achieved by being consistent doing the right things. The servant who doubled his five talents was commended by his master for being faithful in:

*Matthew 25:21*

*His lord said unto him, Well done, thou good and faithful servant: thou hast been faithful over a few things, I will make thee ruler over many things: enter thou into the joy of thy lord.*

*Revelation 2:10*

*Fear none of those things which thou shalt suffer: behold, the devil shall cast some of you into prison, that ye may be tried; and ye shall have tribulation ten days: <u>be thou faithful unto death, and I will give thee a crown of life.</u>* (Underline mine)

The above scripture tells us that those who are faithful unto death will be given a crown of life. Therefore, we are to be faithful both to God and men.

## 2 Chronicles 25:1-2

¹ *Amaziah was twenty and five years old when he began to reign, and he reigned twenty and nine years in Jerusalem. And his mother's name was Jehoaddan of Jerusalem.*

² *And he did that which was right in the sight of the LORD, <u>but not with a perfect heart.</u>* (Underline mine)

2 Chronicles 25:2 - New King James Version (NKJV)

"*And he did what was right in the sight of the LORD, <u>but not with a loyal heart.</u>*" (Underline mine)

How do you do the things you do for God and men? King Amaziah did the right things but not with a perfect, loyal, or faithful heart. Did he do the right things? Yes! How? Not with a loyal or faithful heart. He probably did the right things while grumbling, deceptively, unhappily, and treacherously. To God, that is unsatisfactory. That's why the Bible recorded it for us to know the state of his heart when he did the right things. God knows the heart of every man. He tries our hearts and reins. God looks at man inwardly, but men look outwardly – See 1 Samuel 16:7, and Jeremiah 17:9-10. You may fool men and get away with it but not God. God knows when we accomplish our tasks with integrity and a loyal heart. This is indeed what earns us a promotion from God.

The issue of faithfulness starts from yourself. Do you realize that if you don't keep up with your personal plans, goals, values, pledges etc, you are unfaithful to yourself? What did you decide you will be doing consistently for yourself that you have stopped doing as you planned? Have enough self-discipline to be faithful to yourself, otherwise you will also be disloyal to other people. Extend your loyalty to your partner, family, church, employer, community, and the entire society. Jesus asked this powerful question in:

## Luke 16:12

*And if ye have not been faithful in that which is another man's, who shall give you that which is your own?*

In the world, people sort of find it hard to do voluntary work, or support another organisation. They want to make money, and be their own boss. But Jesus asked this powerful question, *"And if ye have not been faithful in that which is another man's, who shall give you that which is your own?"* This means that if you desire to have your own company, ministry, or whatever, you've got to be faithful in supporting another man or company. You've got to be faithful in your present company, ministry, business, etc because if you are not, Jesus asked, who will give you your own? The answer is NOBODY! Pass the test of being loyal in another man's organisation. The more faithful we are, through the power of the Holy Spirit, the more Christ-like we become.

## Proverbs 20:6

*Most men will proclaim every one his own goodness: but a faithful man who can find?*

Just like Jesus, King Solomon also asked this powerful question, *"but a faithful man who can find?"* If it was easy to find faithful men, he wouldn't be asking that question. They are rare to find, and that ought not to be so. As a Christian, you have to deliberately, and intentionally begin to work on yourself as you also connect to the power of the Holy Spirit to be a faithful child of God.

Many Christians love the blessings of the Lord but they don't all realize that faithfulness is one of the main attributes we need to have blessings. Read how King Solomon, the wisest man that ever lived put it in:

## Proverbs 28:20

*A faithful man shall abound with blessings:*
*but he that maketh haste to be rich shall not be innocent.*

The above scripture states that, *"A faithful man shall abound with blessings:"* Logically, an unfaithful man shall abound with curses, and poverty. Can you see the relationship between faithfulness and blessings? The more faithful we are, through the power of the Holy Spirit, the more Christ-like we become.

## *Meekness*

Meekness, or gentleness is the ability to be quiet, submissive, and humble. Moses was described as the meekest man on earth in *Numbers 12:3* that says, *"(Now the man Moses was very meek, above all the men which were upon the face of the earth.)"* Anytime you want to know what a meek man looks like, picture Moses in your mind, and you can even study him as a character in the Bible. The meeker we are, through the power of the Holy Spirit, the more Christ-like we become.

## *Temperance*

Temperance, or self-control is the ability to control yourself from bad emotions, desires, and vices. Examples are anger, bitterness, lust, greed, covetousness, envy, jealousy, gossip, hatred, pride etc. As you grow in the fruit of the Spirit, these vices will also gradually die. Self-discipline, and self-restraint are also closely related to temperance.

## 1 Corinthians 9:27

<u>*But I keep under my body, and bring it into subjection*</u>*: lest that by any means, when I have preached to others, I myself should be a castaway.* (Underline mine)

Apostle Paul says in the above scripture that he disciplines his body by bringing it into subjection. Another translation says he buffets his body. It's your flesh, therefore, determine that you will not allow your flesh rule over your spirit. Fast and do other spiritual exercises to be in the Spirit allowing the Holy Spirit to impart and interact with your spirit smoothly. The more we have self-control over vices, through the power of the Holy Spirit, the more Christ-like we become.

# CHAPTER TWELVE

# INTIMACY WITH THE HOLY SPIRIT

As a Christian walking with the Holy Spirit consistently over time, the stage of intimacy with the Holy Spirit will require a much deeper dimension such that you will be a lot more fused, and united together with Him as you fellowship and commune regularly with Him. You will be operating on the same frequency level with the Holy Spirit as you align with Him. This is the stage where you now carry His presence and glory with you and manifest it anywhere you appear as an ambassador of Jesus Christ. This is the stage where the Holy Spirit becomes a lot more real as a person to you than ever because you can perceive more of His presence. You can talk, laugh, and feel His presence.

The presence of God produces victory, restoration, and glory. And glory is heavy. That's why God will take you through a process during intimacy for you to have experiential knowledge of certain things that will be released to you in advance.

Before a person will attain to the level of communing intimately with the Holy Spirit, they would have been through a process. This includes being born again, having indwelling of the Holy Spirit, water baptism, infilling of the Holy Spirit, and the Holy Spirit empowerment.

Let me give you an analogy to illustrate what I have just said about undergoing a process. When an airplane is scheduled for a flight, does it start flying straightaway? No! The pilot of the airplane will first start the engines, go on the runway, start increasing the speed of the airplane gradually and then very fast building up momentum, and then lift off the ground to get to a high altitude where it can start flying. That's how walking intimately with the Holy Spirit can also be. You start off in the flesh, and then grow and mature through regular spiritual exercises to the point where you live in the Spirit. *Galatians 5:25, says, "If we live in the Spirit, let us also walk in the Spirit." Romans 8:9 also says, "But ye are not in the flesh, but in the Spirit, if so be that the Spirit of God dwell in you. Now if any man have not the Spirit of Christ, he is none of his."*

Let's look at some examples of individuals who had an intimate relationship with the Holy Spirit as a way of demonstrating this intimacy.

## Old Testament

### King David

King David had a very good relationship with the Holy Spirit of God. This made him an outstanding king, warrior, psalmist, and prophet of God. He valued the Holy Spirit so much that he prayed to God that He should not take the Holy Spirit from him.

*Psalms 51:11*

*Cast me not away from thy presence; and take not thy holy spirit from me.*

King David was ready to forfeit everything but not the Holy Spirit because he now communes with Him at a very intimate dimension. He so much communes with God to the extent that God said this about him in:

*Acts 13:22*

*And when he had removed him, he raised up unto them David to be their king; to whom also he gave testimony, and said, <u>I have found David the son of Jesse, a man after mine own heart, which shall fulfil all my will</u>.* (Underline mine)

God tries the hearts and reins of every man. And for Him to make the underlined statement in the above scripture that King David is a man after His own heart shows that King David truly spends time in isolation to commune with God to have such level of intimacy. Intimacy with the Holy Spirit is highly characterized by isolation to be alone with Him. We see that with King David a lot as he prays and cries out to God in the book of Psalms. The first time Prophet Samuel came to Jesse's house to anoint the next king who will replace King Saul in 1 Samuel 16, the whole family was at home except David who was alone looking after his father's flock. When King Saul was after him, he was in many wildernesses alone. For example, he was in the wilderness of Ziph, Maon, Engedi, Paran, and Ziklag just to mention some. He was also in cave adullam. What was David doing in all these places? Communing with God.

Intimacy with the Holy Spirit requires a genuine sacrifice of your time alone with Him. This is not negotiable. God is a Spirit, and they that worship Him must worship Him in Spirit and in truth.

Intimacy requires your total surrender. You have to be prepared to surrender your own will to the Holy Spirit as He imparts you. All your focus must be on Him. No distractions. At this point, your problems and challenges will be insignificant, and irrelevant. And the Holy Spirit will supernaturally take care of any issues arising as you focus on Him. For example, health, financial, family, ministry etc issues will be taken care of. *Matthew 6:8* says, *"Be not ye therefore like unto them: for your Father knoweth what things ye have need of, before ye ask him."*

## Job

Job is another man who had an intimate relationship with God. He is a character worthy of emulation. This is how the Bible described him in:

## Job 1:1-3

*¹ There was a man in the land of Uz, whose name was <u>Job</u>; and that man was <u>perfect and upright</u>, and one that <u>feared God, and eschewed evil</u>.*

*² And there were born unto him seven sons and three daughters.*

*³ His substance also was seven thousand sheep, and three thousand camels, and five hundred yoke of oxen, and five hundred she asses, and a very great household; <u>so that this man was the greatest of all the men of the east.</u>* (Underline mine)

Job was described in the above scriptures as a perfect and upright man who feared God and hated evil, and was the greatest or wealthiest man in the east. Unfortunately, Satan struck this man, and he lost everything he had in one day. Yes, everything! Now read what the Bible says about Job's reaction to his great loss.

*Job 1:22 - In all this Job sinned not, nor charged God foolishly.*

## The Bible says again in:

## Job 2:7-10

*⁷ So went Satan forth from the presence of the LORD, and smote Job with sore boils from the sole of his foot unto his crown.*

*⁸ And he took him a potsherd to scrape himself withal; and he sat down among the ashes.*

*⁹ Then said his wife unto him, Dost thou still retain thine integrity? curse God, and die.*

*¹⁰ But he said unto her, Thou speakest as one of the foolish women speaketh. What? shall we receive good at the hand of God, and shall we not receive evil? In all this did not Job sin with his lips.*

Verse 7 above tells us that Satan further struck Job with sores all over his body. And his wife said in verse 9, *"Then said his wife unto him, Dost thou still retain thine integrity? curse God, and die."* Read verse 10 above for Job's answer.

Job held on to God in good and bad times. He retained his integrity before God. He did not complain or blame God. He judged God faithful and righteous in all situations. This is real intimacy with God and the Holy Spirit. Your intimacy with the Holy Spirit should not only be in good times. No! It has to be at all times. Job said in:

## Job 13:15

*Though he slay me, yet will I trust in him: but I will maintain mine own ways before him.*

Real intimacy is to trust God at all times. God was pleased with Job's integrity and He rewarded him. Read this:

## Job 42:10

*And the LORD turned the captivity of Job, when he prayed for his friends: also the LORD gave Job twice as much as he had before.*

God is a rewarder of them who diligently seek Him. God turned the captivity of Job and gave him double blessings. Job had to pass the test of continued trust and faithfulness before he was rewarded. Learn a lesson here. Don't let anything whatsoever discourage you to stop having intimacy with the Holy Spirit.

**Moses**

Moses had an intimate relationship with God. God chose him to be the leader for the Israelites. Moses wrote the first five books of the Bible called *Torah*[15] in Hebrew, and *Pentateuch*[16] in Greek. As a leader, he depended on God's presence, guidance, and directions.

*Exodus 33:12-15*

¹² *And Moses said unto the LORD, See, thou sayest unto me, Bring up this people: and thou hast not let me know whom thou wilt send with me. Yet thou hast said, I know thee by name, and thou hast also found grace in my sight.*

¹³ *Now therefore, I pray thee, if I have found grace in thy sight, shew me now thy way, that I may know thee, that I may find grace in thy sight: and consider that this nation is thy people.*

¹⁴ <u>*And he said, My presence shall go with thee, and I will give thee rest*</u>*.*

¹⁵ <u>*And he said unto him, If thy presence go not with me, carry us not up hence*</u>*.* (Underline mine)

In the above scriptures, Moses asked for God's presence, and directions to lead the people. God agreed saying in verse 14, "*And he said, My presence shall go with thee, and I will give thee rest.*" God agreed because Moses had an intimate relationship with Him. When you have an intimate relationship with the Holy Spirit, He will be glad to grant your prayer requests, His presence, rest, and glory.

## Enoch

*Genesis 5:24*

*And Enoch walked with God: and he was not; for God took him.*

The above scripture tells us that Enoch walked with God and was not because God took him. The man did not die. There was no grave on earth. He translated to the heavens to be with the Lord. He walked with God means he was obedient and reverent to the Lord through intimate relationship. This is how the Bible put it in:

## Hebrews 11:5

*By faith Enoch was translated that he should not see death; and was not found, because God had translated him: for before his translation he had this testimony, that he pleased God.*

Love God, be obedient to the Word of God, and always please Him, and this will certainly pave the way for divine connections and intimacy. Enoch pleased God! Who are you pleasing? Always please God! Always make Him your number one!! Reverence and honor Him above all things and everyone!!!

## New Testament
## Apostle Paul

The great Apostle was not one of the original 12 Apostles that walked directly with our Lord Jesus Christ, yet God used him to do incredible things because he had an intimate relationship with God. Apostle Paul had so many revelations to the extent that he single handedly wrote about two thirds of the entire New Testament epistles. And he wrote some of them while in prison. This great Apostle of God planted many churches, and made many missionary trips across different nations preaching the gospel. He had genuine intimacy with the Holy Spirit. Great results.

## Philippians 3:10

<u>*That I may know him*</u>*, and the power of his resurrection, and the fellowship of his sufferings, being made conformable unto his death;* (Underline mine)

After the Apostle Paul had walked with God for many years, with so many revelations, he was still humble enough to make the above statement, *"That I may know him…"* This shows there is no end to having an intimate relationship with the Holy Spirit. Keep going deeper and deeper to know Him.

## Evidence that you are having an intimate relationship with the Holy Spirit

*Vices are effectively dealt with*: You will discover certain vices like anger, bitterness, unforgiveness, lust, greed, covetousness, hatred, envy, jealousy, pride, impatience etc has unknowingly been dealt with through your intimate relationship with the Holy Spirit. A lot of bad habits and character will disappear from you because they have been starved for a long time. The Holy Spirit works in you, and through you to make you to be Christ-like.

*You become Christ-like*: Another proof that you have been long enough with the Holy Spirit in isolation is that you will take on His characteristics, features, and qualities. You will smell, talk, think, and act like Him. For example, when somebody stays in a factory where they make Hugo Boss perfumes for a long time, they will come out smelling Hugo Boss perfume. Similarly, when you stay a long time alone with the Holy Spirit, you will carry His presence and release the smell of His attractive fragrance.

*Constant communication:* You will be in constant communication with the Holy Spirit as a sign of intimacy with Him. You wake up in the morning, and you will greet Him saying, "Good morning Holy Spirit. Thank you for waking me up. Thank you for excellent health. I am grateful for your provisions and support. Fill me with your anointing and presence. Fill my home with your presence. Holy Spirit, you are welcome. I love you, Spirit of the living God. Have mercy on me and my family. Fill me to overflow with your wisdom, anointing, love, joy, peace, and grace. Empower me, strengthen me, and make me whole. I love you Holy Spirit."

*Fear dies*: As you continue your intimacy with the Holy Spirit, a lot of challenges will be dealt with without you even being aware. You are not scared of the enemies knowing that the Lord will fight for you and you will hold your peace. The battle is the Lord's. The Bible says in: *Psalms 3:6, "I will not be afraid of ten* thousands of people, that have set themselves against me round about." The Word of God says again in: *Psalms 23:4*, *"Yea, though I walk through the valley of the shadow of death, I will fear no evil: for thou art with me; thy rod and thy staff they comfort me."*

*Joy*: As you continue to have an intimate relationship with the Holy Spirit, the joy of the Lord will fill you up and strengthen you. The Bible says in: *Psalms 16:11*, *"Thou wilt shew me the path of life: in thy presence is fullness of joy; at thy right hand there are pleasures for evermore."* The Bible says again in: *Philippians 4:4*, *"Rejoice in the Lord alway: and again I say, Rejoice."* And then, 1 Peter 1:8 says, *"Whom having not seen, ye love; in whom, though now ye see him not, yet believing, ye rejoice with joy unspeakable and full of glory:"*

*Peace*: Peace is precious and priceless. Your intimacy with the Holy Spirit will envelop you with internal and external peace. *Philippians 4:7* says, *"And the peace of God, which passeth all understanding, shall keep your hearts and minds through Christ Jesus."*

*More wisdom, anointing, love, and fullness of God*: Your consistent intimacy with the Holy Spirit will produce more wisdom, anointing, and fullness of God. You will have more light, illumination, and revelations from the Word of God, and manifesting more of the love of Christ. The Bible says in: *Ephesians 3:19*, *"And to know the love of Christ, which passeth knowledge, that ye might be filled with all the fulness of God."* Hallelujah!

*Keeping up intimacy with the Holy Spirit*: This is a word of caution. In order to have a consistent intimacy with the Holy Spirit, you must keep doing the things you did that brought you to that deeper dimension. If you stop doing them, the power and glory of the Holy Spirit will also start dwindling. For example, you must not get to the point that you are too busy with work, events, and activities that you no longer isolate yourself to spend time with the Holy Spirit.

You've done well reading this book. My prayer for you is 1 Thessalonians 5:23:

*"And the very God of peace sanctify you wholly; and I pray God your whole spirit and soul and body be preserved blameless unto the coming of our Lord Jesus Christ."* God bless you abundantly in Jesus' name. Amen!

## *2 Corinthians 13:14*

*"The grace of the Lord Jesus Christ, and the love of God, and the communion of the Holy Ghost, be with you all. Amen."*

# SPREAD THE GOOD NEWS

Well-done! You have successfully finished reading this book, I believe you must have picked up some principles that will help you grow in the Word of God, and spiritually as you apply them in your life. It is the application of the principles you have learnt that will bring about a transformation in your life and also give you your desired results. So, keep on practicing what you have learnt.

Now that you have read this book, and you are blessed, I would like you to tell your family, friends, and colleagues about it and spread the good news of the principles you have learnt. Recommend this book to at least twenty people you know, and you can even get some copies for your loved ones as a gift. As you do this, you become a blessing to others and also enlighten the world from where you are. Thank you and God bless you abundantly.

MICHAEL NWADUBA

# BIBLIOGRAPHY

1. The Holy Bible containing the Old and New Testaments. Authorized King James Version. Reference Edition. Thomas Nelson Bibles, A Division of Thomas Nelson, Inc. Copyright 1989 Thomas Nelson Inc. Printed in the United States of America.
2. The Living Bible. Parents Resource Bible. A Life Application Bible. Edysyl Publications. Parents Resource Bible. Copyright 1995 by Tyndale House Publishers.
3. The Amplified Bible. Copyright 1954, 1958, 1962, 1964, 1965, 1987 by The Lockman Foundation.
4. The Thompson Chain-Reference Study Bible. Second Improved Edition. New International Version. Copyright 1973, 1978, 1984 by International Bible Society.
5. Graham, Billy. *The Holy Spirit*. Zondervan. 1978.
6. Meyer, Joyce. *Knowing God Intimately*. Hatchet Books Group. 2015.
7. Cho, Paul Y. *The Holy Spirit My Senior Partner*. Creation House. 1989.
8. Copeland, Gloria. *Walking With God*. Kenneth Copeland Publications. 1995.
9. Torrey, R.A. *The Presence & Work of the Holy Spirit*. Whitaker House. 1996.
10. Hagin, Kenneth E. *The Holy Spirit and His Gifts*. Rhema Bible Church. 1974.
11. Kuhlman, Kathryn. *The Greatest Power in the World*. Kathryn Kuhlman Foundation. 1997.
12. Prince, Derek. *The Holy Spirit in You*. Whitaker House. 1987.
13. Murray, Andrew. *Experiencing the Holy Spirit*. Christian Art Publishers. 2005.

14. Chavda, Mahesh & Bonnie. *Getting to Know the Holy Spirit.* Chosen Books. 2011.

15. Smith, Alice. *Spiritual Intimacy with God.* Bethany House Publishers. 2008.

16. Rogers, Adrain. *The Power of His Presence.* Crossway Books. 1995.

17. Vine, W.E. *Vine's Complete Expository Dictionary of Old and New Testament Words.* Thomas Nelson Publishers. 1984, 1996.

18. Youngblood, Ronald F. (Gen. Editor), Bruce F.F. & Harrison R.K. (Consulting Editors). *New Illustrated Bible Dictionary.* Thomas Nelson Publishers. 1995, 1986.

**NOTES:** (Vine, W.E. *Vine's Complete Expository Dictionary of Old and New Testament Words.* Thomas Nelson Publishers. 1984, 1996. pp. 113–114, 210–213 – *Qados*)[1] (Ibid. pp. 307, & 545–546 – *Hagiasmos & Hagiazo*)[2-3] (Ibid. pp. 240–241 – *Ruah*)[4] (Ibid. pp. 79, 593, & 677 – *Pneuma*)[5] (Ibid. pp. 110–111 – *Parakletos*)[6] (Ibid. pp. 115, 233 *Koinonia*)[7] (Ibid. p. 50 – *Baptisma & Baptizo*)[8-9] (Ibid. p. 636 – *Glossa*)[10] (Ibid. pp. 382–383 – *Agape*)[11] (Ibid. pp. 335–336 – *Chara*)[12] (Ibid. pp. 173–174 – *Salom*)[13] (Ibid. p. 464 – *Eirene*)[14] (Ibid. pp. 133–134 – *Torah*)[15] (Ibid. p. 74 – *Pentateuch*)[16]

*All scriptural references in this book are taken from the King James Version except where indicated.*

# FOR INFORMATION, ENQUIRIES, OR BOOKINGS TO SPEAK

Please send all correspondence directly to:

Email: mikenwaduba@gmail.com

# OTHER BOOKS WRITTEN BY THE AUTHOR

1. A Simple Guide for Bible Study.
2. Questions and Answers on Tithes: Covenant of Prosperity.
3. Amazing Grace in Abundance
4. Mr and Mrs Evans' Honeymoon on the Island of Majorca, Spain.
5. Healing Balm for the Soul.

To order the above books log into: *www.Amazon.co.uk*

# ABOUT THE AUTHOR

 Michael Nwaduba is a Minister of God with a calling to write and evangelise. Prior to God's calling into ministry, he obtained qualifications in Business Administration, and Accountancy. He worked for nearly two decades as a finance officer for various establishments including being a Church Administrator for a Pentecostal Church in London.

He teaches the truth in the Word of God with a passion. He firmly believes in the integrity of the Word of God. You will find his books interesting and easy to understand because of the simple style he adopts as an author. You will also find biblical and practical life examples in his books.

Minister Mike is also a lawyer. He obtained his LLB (Hons) Law degree from London South Bank University, London, United Kingdom. He is a member of RCCG Victory House, London, and the former Personal Assistant (PA) to Pastor Leke Sanusi, Special Assistant to The General Overseer (SATGO), RCCG Europe Mainland Region 2.

www.ingramcontent.com/pod-product-compliance
Lightning Source LLC
LaVergne TN
LVHW041613070426
835507LV00008B/210